TOBRUK
1941

TOBRUK
1941

PIER PAOLO BATTISTELLI

First published 2012
by Spellmount, an imprint of
The History Press
The Mill, Brimscombe Port
Stroud, Gloucestershire, GL5 2QG
www.thehistorypress.co.uk

British Library Cataloguing in Publication Data.
A catalogue record for this book is available from the British Library.

ISBN 978 0 7524 6878 5

Typesetting and origination by The History Press
Printed in Malta
Manufacturing managed by Jellyfish Print Solutions Ltd

CONTENTS

ACKNOWLEDGEMENTS

The author wishes to thank Dr Christopher Pugsley, Royal Military Academy Sandhurst and the series editor Jo de Vries for their help and support. Thanks also to the following for their help in securing sources and photos: Lieutenant Colonel Filippo Cappellano (Rome), Professor Piero Crociani (Rome), Dr Andrea Molinari (Milan) and Count Ernesto G. Vitetti (Rome).

LIST OF ILLUSTRATIONS

33 A German Panzer IV tank moving past a destroyed Bren Gun Carrier.

34 A German Panzer III command tank, used either by the 5th or 8th Panzer Regiment's headquarters.

35 Rommel pointing something out to his staff.

36 German Panzers and armoured cars advancing.

37 A Crusader tank moving past a burning German Panzer IV tank.

38 Generals Charles Norrie and Neil Ritchie.

39 Afrika Korps' soldiers in a typical battle scene.

40 Bren Gun Carriers of the 7th Armoured Division, the 'Desert Rats'.

41 Generals Bernard Freyberg VC and Claude Auchinleck.

42 A German Fieseler Storch (stork) reconnaissance plane has landed close to a motorised column of the Afrika Korps.

43 Armour of the Italian Ariete Division moving in open desert.

44 A German half-tracked SdKfz 250/3 command vehicle, mostly used for communications and observation purposes.

45 General Erwin Rommel, who since August 1941 commanded the Panzer Group Afrika, along with his chief of staff, General Alfred Gause (left).

46 The commander-in-chief Middle East, General Sir Claude Auchinleck, with his chief of staff, General Neil Ritchie, who replaced Cunningham as Eighth Army's commander on 26 November 1941.

47 An Australian 'digger' helps a wounded Italian prisoner of war to the truck that will take him and his comrades to the POW camp.

48 Italian prisoners of war are being escorted to a POW camp.

49 A German column on the move.

50 Close inspection of a destroyed German Panzer IV tank.

INTRODUCTION

When war broke out in Europe in September 1939, the Mediterranean had not been considered to be of significant strategic value. From France and Great Britain's point of view, there was little, if any, reason to be concerned about the area, as the Axis countries, Germany and Italy, were mainly focused on fighting a war in Europe and the African colonies – territory which Germany had lost at the end of the First World War. Also, if Italy was to enter the war on the side of her German ally, it was much more likely to become a burden, rather than an asset, as Italy would have needed to be supplied with the raw materials essential for a modern war, including oil, steel and coal. Strategically speaking, Italy's position in the Mediterranean (bombastically considered the *Mare Nostrum*, 'our sea') was extremely difficult; the country extends far into the sea, which made it a sort of natural aircraft carrier, and the Italian Navy was inferior to both the French and the British navies in the area. Even Italy's colonies were in an awkward strategic position; Libya, with a Mediterranean coastline of 1,770km, was surrounded to the south and west by French colonies, and by the British-held Egypt and Sudan to the east. Similarly, the other Italian colony in Africa, Italian East Africa, was trapped between the Red Sea, the Indian Ocean and surrounded by British colonies to the north, south and west.

Before the war there had been discussions and plans in Italy concerning a possible solution to this strategic impasse. The primary aim was to seize Egypt with a massive land offensive from Libya, and to link up with the colony in Italian East Africa; however, the Italian Navy cut the discussions short by declaring that, given the superiority of the French and British navies in the area, it would be impossible to supply Libya from the mainland, making any offensive plans redundant. When Italy entered the Second World War on 10 June 1940, her strategy in the area was strictly defensive; her colonies were asked to resist any attack by the enemy and to hold out as long as possible. However, events in Europe were quick to alter the strategic settings in the Mediterranean. On 10 May 1940 the German offensive in Western Europe started, and in a matter of weeks it was clear that the Allies were facing defeat; Holland was the first to surrender, followed by Belgium, while French and British forces were surrounded at Dunkirk. A few days after the pocket was evacuated from the beaches, the German offensive against central and southern France started, leading to her surrender on 22 June 1940.

With the fall of France, the strategic situation in the Mediterranean had completely changed; the Royal Navy no longer had superiority over the Italian Navy, which was now able to supply Libya and thus threaten British supremacy in Egypt. In the summer of 1940 Great Britain was facing two major threats: the seaborne invasion of the British Isles by German forces on the west coast of France, and the Italian threat against the British territories in north-west Africa and the Middle East. Although lacking the epic quality of the Battle of Britain, the outcome of the war in the Mediterranean was also decided by narrow margins. Nevertheless, their superiority notwithstanding, the Italians sat idle and waited for Germany to defeat Great Britain; the island of Malta was not seized and the offensive against Egypt was late to start. The offensive only took place in September 1940, lasted a few days and halted at Sidi Barrani, well short of the first main objective of Mersa Matruh. About one month later Italy attacked Greece in an ill-fated venture, thus turning the tide of the war in the Mediterranean herself.

12

The Italian-Greek war soon turned into a quagmire, absorbing large numbers of the Italian forces and adding further distraction from Egypt and the Mediterranean, while the Germans, who had their own road to the Mediterranean barred by Mussolini's ambitions, were unable to intervene. Disasters followed one after another; in mid-November the Greeks counterattacked, while the Royal Navy attacked the Italian harbour of Taranto with torpedo planes, putting three Italian battleships out of action and regaining naval superiority. Less than a month after this remarkable achievement, on 9 December 1940, the British forces in Egypt attacked the Italians at Sidi Barrani. Soon, what had been intended as a local counterattack turned into a major offensive that led to the conquest of Libya's eastern region, Cyrenaica,

1. Italian motorcyclists crossing the Libyan–Egyptian border during the short-lived offensive of September 1940, which was to halt at Sidi Barrani.

and to the destruction of the bulk of the Italian forces. Facing no other option, Mussolini had to ask Hitler for help, and he got it in the form of air and land forces, the Afrika Korps. At first only intended to prevent a British seizure of Libya, the Afrika Korps soon turned into a key factor of the war in North Africa and the Western Desert.

Following a familiar pattern, the pendulum of war swung again. On 30 March 1941 the Afrika Korps began its own offensive into Cyrenaica, leading to the key harbour of Tobruk being surrounded on 11 April. Five days previously, the Germans attacked Greece and Yugoslavia, seizing them by the end of the month. In May the Germans conquered the island of Crete, thus putting their air forces within reach of Egypt's main harbour, Alexandria. Once again the British positions in Egypt and the Middle East were threatened, but this time in a far more serious way. There was nothing to prevent the Germans from advancing into Egypt, except one place: Tobruk. Held by Australian troops, it resisted attack for months, thus denying the Axis forces the main supply base for an advance into Egypt. However, it could not be held forever. On 18 November 1941 the newly formed Eighth Army began Operation Crusader, with the aim of relieving Tobruk and driving the Axis forces from Cyrenaica. What followed was the first major battle fought in the Western Desert, and another swing of the pendulum.

TIMELINE

15 September	The Battle of Britain reaches its climax, and Germans admit defeat. German night raids against British cities, the Blitz, begins in October
23–25 September	Failure of de Gaulle's attempt to seize Dakar, Senegal
27 September	Germany, Italy and Japan sign the Tripartite Pact
23 October	Hitler meets General Franco and tries to persuade him to enter the war
27 October	Free French forces in Cameroon attack the Vichy-held colony of Gabon. Vichy forces eventually surrender on 12 November
28 October	Italy attacks Greece; the following day RAF aircraft redeploy to Crete
11 November	Fleet Air Arm attack against Taranto harbour
18 November	Greece counterattack against Italian forces
27 November	Italian-British naval battle at Cape Sparti-vento (Cape Teulada for the Italians)
9 December	British attack against Italian forces at Sidi Barrani, start of Operation Compass
12–15 December	British seizure of Sollum and Halfaya at the Libyan frontier
18 December	Hitler issues his directive for the attack against the Soviet Union, codenamed Operation Barbarossa
3–5 January	Bardia is attacked and seized by British forces
11 January	The German Luftwaffe launches its first attacks after redeployment to Sicily
	The Long Range Desert Force attacks the Italian garrison of Murzuk in the Sahara
19 January	British offensive against Italian East Africa starts
21–23 January	British attack and seizure of Tobruk

1940

1941

Timeline

5–7 February	Battle of Beda Fomm, British defeat of the remnants of the Italian forces in Cyrenaica
6 February	British seizure of Benghazi. Rommel is appointed commander of the German forces in Africa
7 February	The Italian Ariete Armoured Division arrives in Libya
9 February	Genoa is bombarded by the Royal Navy
12 February	General Rommel arrives in Libya; two days later the first German units arrive
19 February	The Afrika Korps is formed
1 March	The oasis of Kufra in the Sahara is seized by Free French forces
5 March	British forces are sent to Greece
9–16 March	Failure of the Italian offensive against the Greek Army in Albania
23 March	Italian garrison of Jarabub in the Sahara surrenders Rommel starts his drive into Cyrenaica
24 March	Afrika Korps seizes El Agheila
28 March	Italian-British naval battle of Cape Matapan
1 April	Afrika Korps seizes Mersa Brega
3 April	Coup d'état in Iraq, British troops withdraw from Benghazi
5 April	British seizure of Addis Ababa in Italian East Africa
6 April	Germany attack against Greece and Yugoslavia
7 April	British Generals Neame and O'Connor are captured; British stand at El Mechili
8 April	Axis advance to El Mechili
10–11 April	Axis forces reach Bardia and Sollum; Tobruk is cut off and besieged
13 April	German forces occupy Belgrade

1941

1941

10–14 April	First Axis attacks on Tobruk
12 April	The Afrika Korps reaches Bardia and the Libyan–Egyptian border
16–17 April	Second Axis attack on Tobruk
19–20 April	British Commando raid on Bardia
21 April	British decision to evacuate Greece; embarkation follows on 24–30 April
27 April	German forces enter Athens
30 April–4 May	Major Axis attack against Tobruk
30 April	Iraqi forces siege the British-held airport of Habbaniya
2 May	British forces attack in Iraq
5–12 May	Passage of 'Tiger' convoy to Egypt
6 May	The bulk of German 15th Panzer Division arrives in Libya
15–17 May	Operation Brevity: British attacks at Sollum, Halfaya and Capuzzo
16 May	The Italian commander in Italian East Africa surrenders to the British forces
20 May	German airborne attack against Crete
27–30 May	British forces advance to Baghdad, the armistice is signed on 31 May
8 June	British and Free French forces enter Syria
15–17 June	Operation Battleaxe: British attack at the Halfaya, Sollum and Capuzzo area on the Libyan–Egyptian frontier
22 June	Germany invades the Soviet Union, start of Operation Barbarossa
5 July	General Wavell is replaced by General Auchinleck at the head of Middle East Command
12 July	General Bastico replaces General Gariboldi as commander-in-chief in Libya

Timeline

14 July	British and Free French occupation of Syria is completed
1 August	The Panzergruppe (Panzer group) Afrika is formed under Rommel's command
19–29 August	First stage of the relief of Australian troops in Tobruk
25 August	British forces enter Persia; Teheran is seized by British and Soviet forces on 17 September
2 September	General Auchinleck issues a preliminary order for Operation Crusader
18 September	Eighth Army is formed
19–20 September	Second stage of the relief of Australian troops in Tobruk
24–26 September	Operation Halberd: British supply convoy to Malta
12–15 October	Third stage of the relief of Australian troops in Tobruk
10–12 November	Operation Perpetual: British supply convoy to Malta; the British aircraft carrier *Ark Royal* is sunk by a German submarine off Gibraltar
16–17 November	British Commando forces launch Operation Flipper, the attempt to kill Rommel, which ends in failure
18 November	Start of Operation Crusader
27 November	The surrender of the last Italian garrison at Gondar puts an end to the campaign in East Africa
7 December	Japanese attack on Pearl Harbor; the United States enter the war
11 December	Germany and Italy declare war on the United States
17–19 December	First naval battle of the Sirte between Italian and British forces; an Italian supply convoy reaches Libya

1941

Tobruk 1941

1942	**19 December**	Italian manned torpedoes attack Alexandria harbour, damaging the battleships *Queen Elizabeth* and *Valiant*. Loss of British naval superiority in the Mediterranean
	2 January	Axis forces at Bardia surrender
	17 January	Axis forces at Sollum and Halfaya surrender
	21 January	Axis forces advance back into Cyrenaica from Mersa Brega to El Agheila
	28 January	British forces evacuate Benghazi and withdraw toward Gazala
	2 February	The Eighth Army stabilises the Gazala–Bir Hakeim line

HISTORICAL BACKGROUND

A decisive factor in the development of the situation in the Western Desert, the area included between Cyrenaica and western Egypt, was the different reactions of the British and Italians to the surrender of France on 22 June 1940. In spite of the direct threat to the British Isles, the strategic importance of the Mediterranean and the Middle East urged the British Middle East commander, General Wavell, to suggest a revision of the situation to the War Cabinet as early as July 1940. The War Cabinet analysis revealed worrying shortages of land and air forces, which was rather serious since an Italian invasion of Egypt was expected at any moment, despite the early British successes against the Italian forces on the Libyan–Egyptian frontier. Air and naval reinforcements were promptly sent, although the strength of land forces could hardly improve given the losses suffered by the British Army in France and the need to keep the whole area under control. The balance of forces was entirely in the Italians' favour, who had about 220,000 troops in Libya which greatly outnumbered the 50,000 under Wavell's command. However, this was mostly just on paper; in fact the Italian Army in Libya was almost entirely made of second-rate units, a direct consequence of the pre-war strategic decision that ruled out any offensive action and turned the whole area to the defensive.

Only nine out of the fourteen Italian divisions in Libya were made of regular infantry, but they lacked the mobility essential for desert warfare because, although motor transport was available, each division did not have its own. The situation was not much better for the other three 'Blackshirt' divisions, which were made of personnel belonging to the fascist militia. Though similar to Hitler's SS, they were anything but elite units and consisted of aged soldiers made available by the army, and also lacked weapons and equipment. Lastly, there were two Libyan divisions recruited in the area, but these were certainly much more suitable for colonial warfare than for a modern war. This was to become the biggest drawback in the Italian strategy during the early stages of the war in the Western Desert, alongside the death of Field Marshal Italo Balbo on 28 June 1940, caused by friendly fire against his aircraft, and his replacement with Field Marshal Rodolfo Graziani, then chief of staff of the Italian Army. A veteran of the Italian colonial wars in Libya and East Africa, Graziani suffered from post-traumatic stress disorder after a bomb attack during his governorship of the newly conquered Italian East Africa, which surely did not help to make up for his other shortcomings. A great organiser, he also took too much time to prepare his campaigns, which were based on the same step-by-step approach used by Kitchener in his Sudan campaign in the late nineteenth century. This could have been a sound approach twenty years before, but it certainly did not take into account the most recent developments in warfare.

ITALIAN BLACKSHIRTS

Six Blackshirt divisions were formed from the fascist militia for the first time in 1935 during the campaign in Ethiopia, before being subsequently disbanded. Another four were formed in 1939, with one division being disbanded before June 1940 and used to bring the others up to strength.

2. Libyan soldiers have taken up position behind a dune. The Italians still relied heavily on these units, with two Libyan divisions spearheading their advance into Egypt in September 1940.

Mussolini's politics and strategy in the summer of 1940 did not help to alleviate the Italian shortcomings either. Sure that the British defeat was only a matter of time, he focused on his own European objectives and neglected the war in the Western Desert. Reinforcements were sent in a piecemeal fashion, consisting mostly of medium tank battalions, while the bulk of the Italian armoured and mobile forces were held in reserve ready to attack Yugoslavia and Greece. Mussolini asked Graziani to invade Egypt, but this was more of a gesture for no one believed a real invasion was necessary in view of the impending British defeat. Graziani's well-prepared offensive started on 13 September 1940 with two Libyan divisions in the lead, followed by a Blackshirt division and two infantry divisions. On the 14th, the British forces withdrew and the Italians continued their steady advance (mainly on foot), approaching Sidi Barrani on the 15th. On the 16th an Italian tank column approached the town, facing no opposition, and an Italian Blackshirt division occupied it during the night. By 18 September the Italian advance came to a halt, having reached its objective with the loss of some ninety dead and 270 wounded. True to the spirit of colonial warfare, Graziani soon turned Sidi Barrani into a stronghold and started to reorganise his troops while supplies were stored for the next leap forward.

About the same time that Graziani had advanced to Sidi Barrani, the Germans faced defeat in the Battle of Britain and started to look elsewhere for an alternative strategy. On 4 October Hitler met Mussolini and suggested a possible strategy against Britain in the Mediterranean, which included the deployment of a German Panzer division to Libya to support the Italian offensive into Egypt. It was only at this point that the Western Desert became a priority for Mussolini, who urged Graziani to move forward to Mersa Matruh in order to create the premise (political and strategic) for a major offensive against the British positions in North Africa and the Middle East. Graziani refused to move forward before supply stocks were completed, and Mussolini's ill-fated decision to attack Greece on 28 October was the first in a series of steps that completely altered the strategic settings in the Mediterranean. Fleet Air Arm's sinking of three Italian battleships in the harbour of Taranto on 11 November was another, while the start of the Greek counteroffensive one week later turned the Italian attack into a disaster and the Italian-Greek war into a battle of attrition. By the end of November, with Graziani's forces still at Sidi Barrani and showing no intention of advancing further, Italian weaknesses became increasingly evident and there were still no signs of German intervention in the Mediterranean.

Since August, British and Commonwealth forces in the Middle East were steadily reinforced both from the United Kingdom and from India; by the end of the year a total of 126,000 troops were brought in, increasing the already available units (British 7th Armoured Division, 6th Australian infantry and 4th Indian infantry divisions) with the British 2nd Armoured Division, plus the 7th Australian, the 5th Indian, the 1st South African and the New Zealand divisions, either complete or with most of their elements. These reinforcements enabled Wavell eventually to develop the plan for the counterblow he had been considering since Graziani's advance to Sidi Barrani in September – a move he deemed

24

ROYAL TANK CORPS AND ROYAL ARMOURED CORPS

The Royal Tank Corps (Royal since 18 October 1923) was formed in July 1917 and, following the creation of the Royal Armoured Corps on 4 April 1939, became the Royal Tank Regiment, with its regiments formed into battalions and absorbed into the RAC.

necessary to face any further advances toward Mersa Matruh. In October, given Italian idleness, the plan developed into a full counteroffensive, although only with the limited aim of regaining the positions at Sidi Barrani and blunting the Italian forces. General O'Connor, the commander of the Western Desert Force, refined the plan and it was approved by General Wavell on 2 November. The counteroffensive, codenamed Operation Compass, was to start with the first suitable moonlight after adequate preparation, particularly with regard to supplies, and was to last for no more than five days.

This was quite a gamble given the balance of forces: the Italians had some 60,000 men at Sidi Barrani, with eighty-two tanks (but only twenty-two medium) and 300 artillery pieces, while O'Connor's Western Desert Force, made up of the 7th Armoured and 4th Indian divisions, had some 36,000 men, with 145 light, eighty medium and forty-eight Matilda tanks, plus some 200 artillery pieces. Clearly O'Connor's forces were more modern than the Italian forces, which included in the Sidi Barrani area the two Libyan divisions, a Blackshirt division and two other infantry divisions.

The last orders were given to O'Connor on 5 December and two days later the troops moved to the assembly areas ready to attack on the 9th. Taken completely by surprise, the Italians offered mixed resistance, but were soon overwhelmed by the far more experienced and aggressive British and Imperial forces. By 11 December all but the remnants of one infantry division, which managed to retreat to

3. Generals Sir Richard O'Connor and Sir Archibald Wavell. O'Connor led the spectacular Operation Compass that soon turned from a local counterattack into a major offensive and a large-scale victory.

the west, had been destroyed. This left O'Connor with an impressive number of prisoners (38,300, at the cost of 624 British and Indian casualties), and huge quantities of weapons, supplies and various other materials were captured. The stunning success led O'Connor, with the approval of Wavell and Churchill, to expand the limited counteroffensive into a major operation, pushing forward to the west despite being told to wait for the 4th Indian Division to be relieved by the 6th Australian Division, with one of its brigades

4. *A British Mk III Valentine infantry tank. Replacing the Matilda in late 1941, it was first used to equip the 8th RTR.*

already on its way. On 10–12 December the Italians practically abandoned Egypt and deployed a Blackshirt division and an infantry division on the Libyan–Egyptian frontier, along with remnants of the troops that had escaped from Sidi Barrani. On 14 December elements of the British 4th Armoured Brigade were already crossing the frontier with the aim of cutting the road between Tobruk and Bardia, but since this may have overextended the supply lines, it was decided to seize the southernmost stronghold along the border, Sidi Omar, which fell on the 16th. At this point Graziani reacted like he was fighting a colonial war, ordering all the Italian troops to withdraw from the frontier and into the fortifications of Bardia and Tobruk. In fact, Graziani (who on the 23rd had replaced the commander of Tenth Army) did consider concentrating all his forces in Tobruk, but Mussolini rejected his proposal since he wanted to keep the enemy forces as far to the east as possible while sending reinforcements. Bardia was held by two Blackshirt and two infantry divisions, with a total of 45,000 troops, 430 artillery pieces, 117 light and thirteen medium tanks.

5. Aerial view of Tobruk on 23 January 1941, after it was seized by Australian troops. The smoke is coming from the burning fuel depots.

O'Connor, who believed there were no more than 10,000 Italians in Bardia, pressed on and attacked on 3 January 1941 with XIII Corps (formed on 1 January from the Western Desert Force). Besieging the fortifications were two Australian brigades supported by the 7th Armoured Division, now with only twenty-three Matilda tanks left; two days later the Italians surrendered with the loss of some 40,000 troops and huge amounts of weapons and supplies, at the cost of 130 killed and 326 wounded on the British and Australian side. On 7 January the Australian spearheads moved from El Adem to the east and surrounded Tobruk. With only 22,000 troops and 340 guns to defend a 54km-long fortified line, there was little hope for the Italians against O'Connor's forces. On 21–22 January the Australians, again supported by the 7th Armoured Division, stormed the fortress and the defenders quickly capitulated. This time 25,000 Italian prisoners were captured, including sailors, plus 208 field guns and eighty-seven tanks, for a total loss of some 400 men from XIII Corps. The city was described by Dr Theodore Stephanides, a medical officer with a Cypriot labour unit: 'At first glance – when seen from distance – Tobruk made a beautiful picture with its flat-roofed, dazzling white houses crowded together on the flank of a low slope overlooking a small landlocked and brilliantly blue bay. What struck me most was the immense amount of Italian shipping sunk in the harbour, masts struck up everywhere out of the water like pins in a pin cushion.'[1] It did not take long for Tobruk's beautiful setting to be decimated by the effects of war.

What was left of the Italian forces in Cyrenaica amounted to about 5,000 troops at Derna and another 14,000 troops, plus 254 guns and fifty-seven medium tanks, deployed between Berta and El Mechili. Against them O'Connor sent two columns, with the 6th Australian Division moving along the coast and 7th Armoured moving inland toward El Mechili and, from there, to the north. The attempt to encircle the Italian armour failed, however, and on 26 January they managed to evade the trap by moving north-west, while the 7th Armoured reached El Mechili the following day. Three days later the Italian garrison of Derna surrendered to the Australians, thus opening the road for the last dash to Benghazi and the gates of Tripolitania. On 1 February Graziani, also concerned by the raid on Murzuk, ordered the withdrawal of what was left of the Tenth Army to the west, while he flew to Tripoli. The following day Royal Air Force reconnaissance spotted the Italian retreat, which compelled O'Connor to alter his plans and prepare the new phase of the advance with supplies and reinforcements, most notably armour from the 2nd Armoured Division to strengthen the fifty Cruiser tanks still in running order with the 7th Armoured. Nevertheless, the advance started on the

---

1   Lyman, R., *The Longest Siege*, pp. 66–7

6. *The downfall: Australian soldiers pose with a portrait of the 'Duce', Benito Mussolini, at Derna shortly after its seizure on 29 January 1940.*

morning of 4 February, British units dashing across some 200km of desert to Beda Fomm, at the bottom of the Cyrenaica bulge.

Advancing along the coast, the Australians seized Benghazi on 6 February, also establishing contact with the 7th Armoured south of the city. Meanwhile, on 5–7 February the last battle was fought at Beda Fomm; British Cruiser tanks of the 4th Brigade, the spearhead of the division, took positions of advantage and started firing on the few Italian medium tanks, destroying them one after another. 'Trooper' Brown recalled, 'Practically all morning we never stopped firing, at wagonloads of infantry or tanks. I haven't a clue how many enemy I killed, but it must have run into hundreds. We

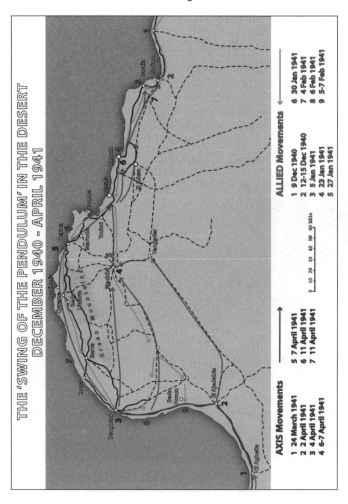

THE 'SWING OF THE PENDULUM' IN THE DESERT
DECEMBER 1940 – APRIL 1941

AXIS Movements

1 24 March 1941
2 2 April 1941
3 4 April 1941
4 6-7 April 1941
5 7 April 1941
6 11 April 1941
7 11 April 1941

ALLIED Movements

1 9 Dec 1940
2 12-15 Dec 1940
3 5 Jan 1941
4 23 Jan 1941
5 27 Jan 1941
6 30 Jan 1941
7 4 Feb 1941
8 6 Feb 1941
9 5-7 Feb 1941

definitely had a score of twenty M13s [medium tanks] at the end of the day …'[2] At the end of the battle there were only twelve Cruiser tanks in running order, but the Italian surrender added another 25,000 prisoners, along with the destruction of at least 100 guns

2 Pitt, B., *Crucible of War I*, p. 180

PANZERS IN AFRICA

In October 1940 Hitler was keen to send one of his Panzer divisions to Libya to support the Italian offensive into Egypt. The 3rd Panzer Division was selected for the purpose and General von Thoma (later becoming commander of the Afrika Korps) went to Libya for an inspection that same month.

7. The 6th Australian Division entering Tobruk, 23 January 1941. In the foreground captured Italian medium tanks marked with large 'Kangaroo' signs to make them easily identifiable.

and 100 tanks. In less than two months, O'Connor's forces had advanced for more than 800km and practically destroyed the bulk of the Italian forces in Libya, taking some 130,000 prisoners, destroying or capturing 845 field guns, more than 200 light and 180 medium tanks, at the cost of 500 killed, 1,373 wounded and fifty-five missing. This was a victory comparable to that of the German Army in Western Europe in May 1940.

Whatever chance O'Connor ever had to advance on Tripoli, it was nullified by other strategic needs. On 11 January 1941 Churchill had ordered Wavell to send troops to Greece, but luckily the talks started two days later in Athens and ended with a Greek refusal. The matter was raised again after the seizure of Benghazi, and this time the Greeks accepted; New Zealand and Australian troops started to be sent to Greece on 5 March, while on 19 January the British offensive against Italian East Africa began. The first Western Desert campaign was over, but the war in this theatre had just begun.

On 9 January 1941 Hitler decided to send German troops to Libya to prevent a British advance to Tripoli and the loss of the Italian colony. An ad hoc unit was formed on 6 February, the 5th Light Division (created from the bulk of the 3rd Panzer Division), and command given to the relatively unknown General Erwin Rommel. Six days later Rommel was in Tripoli, one day after the first convoy carrying German troops had arrived. On 18 February Hitler decided to widen the extent of the German intervention in Libya and ordered a second division, the 15th Panzer Division, to be sent. The following day both divisions were put under the newly formed Afrika Korps, with Rommel at its head. Hitler's decisions seemed to contrast with the British moves, but these were taken with only a limited knowledge of future developments. For example, Hitler knew not only the extent of the German preparations for the invasion of Greece, but also that the invasion of the Soviet Union was to follow shortly thereafter. Thus, from a British perspective the Western Desert was no longer a main theatre of war following the Italian defeat, the decision to support Greece and with the offensive against Italian East Africa already on its way. Conversely, Hitler knew that, no matter what, Greece would not resist for long and the Western Desert would be reinforced and become the only land-based theatre of war where the Axis and the British were to face one another. For the moment, Rommel's orders were quite clear; he was to prevent a British advance on Tripoli, while

AFRIKA KORPS' HERITAGE

Soon after its creation the Afrika Korps inherited the traditions of the German Alpen Korps (Alpine Corps), which fought in the First World War against the Italians. This was done on Hitler's specific request, although the details seem never to have been revealed to the Italians.

building up his own strength and preparing for a major offensive in the autumn. However, Rommel was not your average general.

On 20–21 March Rommel discussed the situation in Africa with Hitler and obtained permission to carry out limited attacks in order to set the basis for the offensive scheduled to take place next autumn. He wasted little time, and on the 31st the 5th Light Division attacked and seized the British 2nd Armoured Division positions at El Agheila. The Germans carried out a reconnaissance in force, seizing Mersa Brega the following day before pushing forward to Agedabia, fighting against British tanks for the first time, or rather Italian medium tanks with British crews. Lieutenant Joachim Schorm of the 5th Panzer Regiment recalled the events: 'Everyone disappears inside the Panzer. The hatches are slammed. Straight ahead. 11 o'clock! High explosive, 1,000 metres. Fire! Bang! A dud! The tracer shells whizz by! Driver overtake! Left steering, brake! In front, behind, to the right and left, the shells burst. High explosive, 800 metres! Same tank. Bang! Too short! But my other tanks have the direction from the impact. Soon the enemy is on fire.'[3]

Facing weak British opposition, the 5th Light Division's commander, General Streich, decided to move the entire division forward and on 2 April seized Agedabia. Rommel then faced strong opposition to any further advance, both from the Italian

---

3 Lyman, *The Longest Siege*, p. 95

commander, General Gariboldi, and from the German high command, which only authorised any further advance if the British began to withdraw from Cyrenaica. Rommel interpreted this as a 'green light' and started his first drive into Cyrenaica with the 5th Light Division, the partly motorised Italian Brescia Division and the Ariete Armoured Division. Facing them were the largely incomplete, and still training, British 2nd Armoured Division, the 3rd Indian Motor Brigade and the weak 9th Australian Division which, given the lack of motor transport, had left one brigade in Tobruk.

On 2 April the 2nd Armoured Division commander, General Gambier-Parry, recognised the threat and ordered a withdrawal to Antelat, but Wavell (who believed that Rommel's offensive was only aimed at Benghazi) ordered the defence of the coastal road too, thus splitting the available forces. On 3 April Rommel decided to launch an offensive aimed at regaining Cyrenaica and had the Italian Brescia Division move along the coastal road with the

8. A German Panzer II tank on a crossroads just outside Agedabia during the early stages of Rommel's drive into Cyrenaica in April 1941.

LIGHT DIVISIONS

The German Army had four light divisions during the Poland campaign in 1939, which consisted of a cavalry regiment and a Panzer battalion. However, having proved mostly ineffective, they were transformed into Panzer divisions soon after the campaign. The 5th Light Division in 1941 retained its original name as it had a distinct organisation.

3rd Reconnaissance Battalion spearheading, while the Italian Ariete Division, supported by the 5th Panzer Regiment, advanced on two routes: along the coastal road until Soluch, before swinging east to Msus, and also deep into the desert east of Antelat, moving toward Maaten el Grara and Bir Tengeder. By 4 April Rommel's spearheads seized Benghazi and advanced to the north-east of Antelat, compelling the British 3rd Armoured Brigade to withdraw and, because of a lack of fuel, practically disintegrate in the process. On the 6th the Axis forces reached El Mechili, against which a major assault was launched the following day after the bulk of the Axis forces had reached the area, defended by the 3rd Indian Motor Brigade. Things took a turn for worse on the British side for, on the 7th, Generals O'Connor and Neame were taken prisoner, while the 9th Australian Division was hurried back to Tobruk. That same day, while El Mechili was heavily attacked, the Brescia Division entered Derna. On 8 April the defenders of El Mechili did try to break away from the attack, but were captured by the Germans. At this point Rommel pushed all his units forward. On 11 April the 9th Australian Division was surrounded at Tobruk, and the following day the German spearheads reached Bardia, eventually breaking though the Libyan–Egyptian frontier on the 24th to Buq-Buq.

In one month Rommel had accomplished his aim, achieving a victory that only differed from O'Connor's campaign in the previous January by the amount of prisoners taken. The victory, however, was incomplete; on 11 April the 8th German Machine Gun Battalion, with the support of twenty-five tanks and ten anti-tank guns, attacked the Tobruk fortified line with great hopes, but unexpected resistance eventually forced the attack to be called back. The following day Rommel tried again, this time his troops moving under cover of a sandstorm, but it soon faltered under heavy artillery fire and was again called back. Rommel was not too worried by the situation and ordered a major attack against the Australian positions to take place on 14 April. He was firmly convinced that the British forces in the Western Desert were too weak to prevent his advance into Egypt, but he did not take into account what was to become a thorn in his side: Tobruk.

THE ARMIES

The Commanders

An interesting feature of the war in the Western Desert was that it exacted an unusually heavy toll on the battlefield commanders of both sides in the first few months. The Italians were, of course, the first and foremost victims: Field Marshal Balbo's accidental death apart, on 3 February 1941 Graziani appointed his chief of staff, General Giuseppe Tellera, to the task of withdrawing the remnants of the Tenth Army west off from Cyrenaica. Tellera was mortally wounded at Beda Fomm, where (amongst several others) another Italian general was captured, Annibale Bergonzoli (nicknamed 'electric whiskers'), who was the commander of XXIII Corps and had previously escaped capture at Bardia and Tobruk. On 11 February 1941 Field Marshal Graziani resigned, the first top brass to fall victim to the war in the Western Desert, and his place at the lead of the Italian troops was taken by General Italo Gariboldi, formerly commander of the Fifth Army in Tripolitania. His clashes with Rommel made this appointment short-lived, and on 12 July 1941 he was replaced by General Ettore Bastico, who remained in command until 1943.

ROMMEL AND THE BRITISH GENERALS

During the Second World War twelve British generals
became prisoners of war on the battlefield: seven in
the Far East, four in the Western Desert (the first ones
being Neame, O'Connor and Gambier-Parry) and one
in France in July 1940 – General Fortune,
who surrendered at Cherbourg to a certain
General Erwin Rommel.

The Allies

The situation was not much better for the British. General
Sir Archibald Wavell, commander-in-chief in the Middle East,
developed a difficult relationship with Churchill and, shortly after
Rommel's drive into Cyrenaica and immediately after the failure of
Operations Brevity and Battleaxe, he was replaced on 5 July 1941
by General Sir Claude Auchinleck. Even the command of British
forces in Egypt was troublesome: the first commander, General
Sir Henry Maitland Wilson, was sent to Greece and replaced
on 4 February 1941 by General Sir Richard Nugent O'Connor,
the famous commander of the Western Desert Force and then
XIII Corps. O'Connor was subsequently captured by the Germans
shortly after the beginning of Rommel's offensive into Cyrenaica,
while General Philip Neame, leading Cyrenaica Command, and
General Michael Gambier-Parry, commander of 2nd Armoured
Division, also suffered the same fate. This led to an almost
immediate reorganisation of the British commands, with General
Marshall-Cornwall taking over British forces in Egypt, Cyrenaica
Command being disbanded and the Western Desert Force being
reconstituted from XIII Corps under the command of General Sir
Noel Beresford-Peirse.

Reorganisation brought no respite for the British commands in
the area. On 18 September Eighth Army was formed under the
command of General Sir Alan Cunningham, with the XIII Corps

Claude Auchinleck

Sir Claude John Eyre Auchinleck was the son of a widowed woman, who raised him in difficult circumstances (this left him with an indifference to personal comfort), and a father with a military background. After attending the Royal Military Academy at Sandhurst, he was commissioned in the Indian Army in 1904 and, during the First World War, served in the Middle East and earned the Distinguished Service Order in 1917. After the war he was stationed in India where he acquired a solid reputation as a soldier. Promoted to major general in 1936, he returned to London in 1939. Sent to Norway in May 1940, he fought at Narvik until the following month when, evacuated back to England, he took over command of IV Corps until November, before he was then sent back to India as commander-in-chief. His direct intervention in Iraq following the insurgency made him the foremost choice to replace Wavell as commander-in-chief Middle East, a position he held until August 1942. Returning to India in 1946 he was promoted to field marshal and was asked to resign the following year, coming back to England where he lived until 1968. He then lived in Marrakech, Morocco, where he died in 1981. A highly controversial character in the context of the Western Desert campaign, Auchinleck was to provide much debate in the post-war period with his decision not to publish his own memoirs, unlike his colleagues, and his actual role in the victory of Operation Crusader and the defeats of 1942.

9. *General Sir Claude Auchinleck (left) and General Sir Archibald Wavell (right), the commanders-in-chief Middle East.*

now under the command of General Alfred Godwin-Austen, and the XXX Corps under the command of General Vyvian Pope, who was killed in an air crash on 5 October 1941 and replaced by General Charles Norrie. Taking a command in the Western Desert continued to be unlucky for subsequent British commanders: Cunningham, Eighth Army commander, was sacked by Auchinleck right in the middle of Operation Crusader and replaced on 26 November by General Neil Ritchie, who was also sacked the following year shortly after Rommel's seizure of Tobruk. Godwin-Austen requested to be replaced at the lead of XIII Corps after Rommel's second drive into Cyrenaica in 1942, practically ending his career, and was replaced by General William Gott, who died in an air crash on 14 August 1942 while taking over command of Eighth Army. Norrie, XXX Corps commander, would also be replaced early in July 1942 following defeat at Tobruk.

The Axis

Impressive though the Italian and British toll may appear, it was nothing compared to the German losses. The first casualty was General Heinrich Kirchheim, a 59-year-old veteran of the German colonies sent to Libya to arrange for the arrival of the Afrika Korps, and given command of a mixed battle group which seized Benghazi. He was wounded on 8 April 1941 approaching El Mechili, although he continued to fight. The first fatality was General Heinrich von Prittwitz, the commander of 15th Panzer Division, killed on 10 April 1941 during the first attack against Tobruk. His successor, General Hans-Karl von Esebeck, was seriously wounded on 13 May at Tobruk and had to be sent back to Europe (he was back on duty in August, but did not return to Africa). His replacement, General Walter Neumann-Silkow, was mortally wounded by British artillery fire on 6 December 1941 near Tobruk. Temporarily replaced by Colonel Erwin Menny, his position was taken by General Gustav von Vaerst on 9 December, himself wounded on 26 May 1942. The battlefield, however, was not the only reason for casualties; after the failure at Tobruk, Rommel started a purge that led to the dismissal of the Afrika Korps' chief of staff, Colonel Klaus von dem Borne, the operations officer, Major Ehlers, and the intelligence officer, Major von Plehwe, who, having already been replaced in March by Captain Wolf von Baudissin, was shot down during a reconnaissance flight over Tobruk on 5 April 1941. Rommel, however, appointed excellent replacements, especially Colonel Fritz Bayerlein as chief of staff of the Afrika Korps, although the purge did not stop there and this was not entirely due to the inadequacy of the German officers serving under the Desert Fox.

The commander of the 5th Light Division, General Johannes Streich, was also relieved along with his Panzer regiment commander. Streich was an irksome character and had clashed with Rommel while in command of the Panzer regiment advancing alongside Rommel's during the May 1940 campaign in Belgium and France; they had been at odds over some bridging equipment which Rommel had taken and never given back. His successor became another battlefield casualty, for General Johann von Ravenstein was captured on 29 November 1941 by New Zealand troops, earning the dubious distinction of being the first German general to suffer this fate in the Second World War. Temporarily replaced by Colonel Gustav-Georg Knabe, command of the renamed 21st Panzer Division was eventually taken over by General Karl Böttcher on 30 November 1941, until then the commander of Rommel's artillery. He eventually fell gravely ill, and had to be replaced himself the next February. The list would not be complete without General Max Sümmermann, the first commander of the 90th Light 'Afrika' Division, who was mortally wounded on 10 December 1941 during an RAF attack. He was temporarily replaced by Colonel Johann Mickl, who managed to escape after capture along with a large group of German soldiers, and eventually reached the German lines after a long walk across the desert. On 28 December 1941, command of the division was taken over by General Richard Veith.

Erwin Rommel

When he was given command of the Afrika Korps in February 1941, Erwin Rommel was still quite an unknown general whose only record had been in command of a Panzer division during the invasion of France in May–June 1940. Born in 1891 to a family without a military background, his attitude was ideal for the armed forces and, after being commissioned in 1910, he was to distinguish himself during the First World War by winning the coveted award of the *Pour le Mérite* (the Blue Max). This enabled him to continue his career in the post-war years, although this was mostly unimpressive except for the publication of his memoirs (*Infantry Attacks*) in 1937. These would attract Hitler's attention, and eventually Rommel became the commander of Hitler's own headquarters until, on his request, he was given command of the 7th Panzer Division in 1940. Rommel was to meet the British troops at Arras during the armoured counterattack of May 1940, displaying personal courage and initiative which helped to blunt and eventually halt it. In February 1941 Hitler initially chose General Streich to command the Afrika Korps, but changed his mind and chose Rommel instead. Commander of the Panzergruppe Afrika since August 1941, Rommel personally led the Axis forces until March 1943 (brief interruptions apart), to become one of the most famous and legendary commanders of the war. He was forced to commit suicide in October 1944 following his alleged role in the July plot to assassinate Hitler.

10. *General Erwin Rommel, who was to acquire the name 'Desert Fox' during the 1941 campaign in the desert.*

ROMMEL'S *POUR LE MÉRITE*

Rommel won his *Pour le Mérite* (also known as the Blue Max) during the early battles that were to lead to the German breakthrough on the Italian front in November 1917, eventually turning into the Italian defeat at Caporetto. He was never to hide this fact from his Italian allies in North Africa.

On 1 August 1941 Rommel took command of the newly formed staff of Panzergruppe Afrika, the Panzer group equivalent to an army command; his place at the lead of the Afrika Korps was taken by General Ludwig Crüwell (himself shot down and captured on 29 May 1942). Rommel's new chief of staff was General Alfred Gause, the leader of an excellent team that included Colonel Siegfried Westphal as operations officer and Major Friedrich Wilhelm von Mellenthin as intelligence officer. They would play a major role during the 'winter battle'.

The Soldiers

The Allied Forces

Largely outnumbered by the Italians, the British Army had one of its finest units in North Africa: the 7th Armoured Division (the 'Desert Rats'), which, along with Commonwealth, Imperial and Dominion troops, would bear the brunt of battle until the very end. Its origins date back to the mechanisation of the Cairo Cavalry Brigade in 1935, two years before the 1st Armoured Division was actually formed in the United Kingdom. Initially composed of three regiments (11th Hussars in armoured cars, 8th Hussars motorised with trucks and 7th Hussars with light tanks), it was soon used to form the 'Matruh Mobile Force', eventually dubbed the 'Immobile Farce'. In 1938 the brigade was reinforced with a tank regiment and a motor infantry battalion, and the 8th Hussars were re-equipped with light tanks, which led the original core of the brigade to be renamed the Light Armoured Brigade. Most important of all, command of the renamed 'Mobile Division Egypt' was taken by Major General Percy Hobart, deservedly considered the most experienced expert in mechanisation. Under Hobart's command the division was to train and develop tactics and procedures not much different from those used by the Germans in Europe, thus becoming the most advanced mechanised unit of the British Army. In February the division was renamed 7th Armoured, now part of O'Connor's Western Desert Force, with Hobart being replaced by General O'Moore Craigh. In November 1940 the 7th Armoured Division was made of two tank brigades (4th and 7th, equipped with Mk VI light tanks, A9 and A10 Cruisers) and a support group, including the 2nd Rifle Brigade, the 1st King's Royal Rifle Corps and the 4th Royal Horse Artillery, plus divisional troops. With the 7th Royal Tank Regiment attached, equipped with Matilda tanks, the division was to spearhead O'Connor's offensive in December 1940 and bring the British advance to its victorious conclusion at Beda Fomm two months later.

Three different factors were to characterise the British war effort in North Africa and the Middle East in 1940–41: first, British Army forces were to represent a minority amongst a majority of Commonwealth and Imperial forces, which was the consequence of the losses suffered in France and of the need to rebuild the British Army extensively. This was also the consequence of the

THE 'IMMOBILE FARCE'

The Matruh Mobile Force came to be known as the 'Immobile Farce' during the 'mobile force exercise' held in 1934. This saw the employment of the 1st Tank Brigade along with the 7th Infantry Brigade, which had been temporarily motorised by pressing civilian motor buses into service.

11. *British infantry during pre-war training in Egypt. Led by General Sir Percy Hobart, the 'Mobile Division Egypt' was renamed the 7th Armoured Division in February 1940.*

common belief that these troops, namely Australians, Indians, South Africans and New Zealanders, were better suited to tropical warfare than the British soldiers, although not before a long period of acclimatisation. The second factor was given by the widespread dispersion of forces during the first six months of war in 1941. This was the result of British strategic and political needs, but it also greatly hampered any opportunity to exploit fully the successes obtained in 1940–41 against the Italians, and created the premise for Rommel's victorious advance into Cyrenaica in March–April 1941. In February–March 1941, forces under British command in the Mediterranean and the Middle East were broken down as follows: the 9th Australian (only partially trained and equipped), the 6th Australian (the 7th was earmarked, but not sent) and the New Zealand divisions were based in Cyrenaica, along with the

Polish Brigade and the bulk of the British 2nd Armoured Division, although one of its brigades was sent to Greece. Another large portion of the forces under Wavell's command fought in Italian East Africa, with the 4th and 5th Indian divisions, plus the 1st, 11th and 12th South African divisions. The third factor was the need to rotate units between the battle front and the rear areas, allowing adequate time for rest and refitting; at the time the 7th Armoured Division was in fact back to Egypt for refitting, thus forming the only available reserve, along with the British 6th Infantry (used as an internal security force) and 1st Cavalry divisions, who were still horse mounted.

Events that followed in the months between March and May 1941 highlighted the weaknesses of the British position in the area; caught in the middle of Rommel's advance into Cyrenaica, the 2nd Armoured Division practically dissolved and was subsequently disbanded. Units deployed in Greece suffered heavy losses, as did the 9th Australian Division at Tobruk, with the consequence that only the New Zealand Division was able to rest and refit in time to take part in Operation Crusader, along with the 4th Indian Division. Both the 6th and 7th Australian divisions were engaged in the Syria campaign, along with the 1st Cavalry, the British 6th Infantry and the 10th Indian Infantry divisions, which, after having fought in Iraq along with the 5th Indian Division, was subsequently employed in the invasion of Persia. Reinforcements took time to be available, with the newly arrived 9th Australian Division not becoming operational for some time. South Africa's decision to impose a restriction on the use of its forces left only the 1st and 2nd South African divisions available, while the British 6th Infantry Division was eventually reorganised to form the 70th Division which, along with the 32nd Army Tank Brigade and the Polish Brigade, did well to relieve the 9th Australian Division at Tobruk.

From January–July 1941 another 239,000 troops arrived in the Middle East to join the 126,000 that had arrived in 1940, thus bringing the Middle East Command to a ration strength of some 336,000. As Churchill was to remark, there was a striking contrast

Eighth Army Soldiers

At the time of Operation Crusader the Eighth Army was still a force primarily made up of Commonwealth and Imperial units, whose differing cultures and battlefield experiences contributed to its shape. The bulk of the army was in fact given by the most experienced unit in the Western Desert, the 7th Armoured Division, although many other units were soon to acquire battlefield experience either in East Africa or Greece. The mixture of nationalities and different backgrounds within the various units forming the Eighth Army was to have its influence in strategy and tactics, but on the field most of these differences would disappear when facing either the hostile environment or the enemy. Soldiers learned how to survive the climate (especially the sudden temperature changes more prominent in Cyrenaica), the plagues of flies and the lack of water, which turned even the smallest wound into an infected 'desert sore', and, above all, how to face the unchanging diet. This was made of meat, vegetables and bully beef, usually mixed with the army biscuits that, though inedible, were often mixed with milk, sugar or jam to produce a porridge known as 'biscuits burgoo'. When out of combat, daily life consisted mostly of routines such as weapons cleaning and vehicle maintenance, with many deprivations and very few comforts, although football and cricket matches were often played by teams from the different corners of the British Empire.

12. An infantry platoon marching past a British Matilda tank. Note how all are wearing the battledress along with the white canvas webbing and gaiters (the second man from the left carries mortar bombs).

ORIENTATION IN THE DESERT

One of the greatest problems faced by soldiers during the Western Desert campaign was orientation, given the almost complete lack of specific and recognisable terrain features that could be used as a reference point. This was particularly true for the Germans, who in 1941 had been trained for warfare in cities and woods.

between overall strength and actual combat strength, which was much lower, and to which Wavell replied that the Middle East was not like Europe and did require a larger amount of service troops. This was true, yet the fact remains that in spite of its numbers, now largely superior to those of the Axis forces (and eventually decisive in the outcome of the battle), Middle East Command suffered from a wide dispersion of its forces and a constant rotation of units, along with the limited availability of British formations which provided the armoured and mechanised core of the army: in November 1941 the Eighth Army only included two British divisions and four brigades (7th Armoured and 70th, 1st and 32nd Army Tank brigades, 4th Armoured Brigade Group and 22nd Guards Brigade Group), the rest being made of troops from the Commonwealth and the Empire (New Zealand, 1st and 2nd South African, 4th Indian divisions), and also the Polish Brigade.

The Axis Forces

This was, however, a much better situation than that of the Italian Army, which was somehow rebuilt and reorganised after the defeats of winter 1940–41. The arrival of the Ariete Armoured Division in February 1941, followed by the motorised Trento and Trieste infantry divisions, brought some much-needed reinforcements after the disastrous defeats and subsequent destruction of ten divisions. This left the Italians with only four infantry divisions;

five after the Trento lost the bulk of its mobile components in the summer–autumn of 1941. These lacked motor transport (the Brescia was only partly and temporarily motorised), and were therefore used to lay siege around Tobruk. Only the Ariete and the Trieste divisions formed the mobile, mechanised force grouped under the Corpo d'Armata di Manovra (Manoeuvre Army Corps, CAM) operating alongside the Afrika Korps. The Italian forces did eventually compensate for Rommel's deficiencies, as although the Afrika Korps was an excellent, mobile fighting force, it required large numbers of men to lay siege to and occupy a city.

Hurriedly formed and sent to Libya as a blocking force, the 5th Light Division had strong tank and anti-tank components, but only two motorised infantry battalions. Lack of naval transport also delayed the arrival of the 15th Panzer Division, which had an entire infantry brigade with five infantry battalions. As a result, in April, a 19,000-strong Afrika Korps besieged 29,000 enemy troops surrounded at Tobruk. The situation improved in the months to follow and by September 1941 the Afrika Korps was 48,500 strong, the peak for that year. A reorganisation also took place within both the 5th Light and 15th Panzer divisions, to coincide with the creation of the Panzergruppe Afrika on 1 August. The 5th Light was renamed 21st Panzer Division and absorbed one infantry battalion and a regimental HQ from the 15th Panzer Division, with the result that the former now had three and the latter four infantry battalions. Infantry was, however, always a critical factor for the Afrika Korps, despite the decision to create the Afrika Division at the end of June, renamed the 90th Afrika Division on 28 November 1941. Again, lack of naval transport delayed its actual formation, which started in mid-to-late October in the Sollum area. The division, which still had a provisional organisation, included a total of eight infantry battalions, partly grouped in two infantry regiments with one containing the only artillery battalion of the division, plus one anti-tank and one engineer battalion for a total strength of about 9,000 troops. This was later increased in the same month to some 13,000 troops by temporarily attaching several units, including the two reconnaissance battalions of both the 15th and 21st Panzer divisions, two anti-aircraft battalions and an artillery battalion.

The Kit

Between June 1940 and February 1942 the war in the Western Desert was fought by soldiers belonging to at least ten different countries (Britain, Germany, Italy, Australia, New Zealand, South Africa, India, Poland, Czechoslovakia and France), not counting the differences existing within each single country, with regional units sometimes attached (given their size) or subordinated to other units and commands. Nevertheless, soldiers fighting in the Western Desert shared many similarities, whether fighting alongside or against each other, than they often did with their comrades fighting in other theatres of war in Europe. Either prior to or upon their arrival in North Africa and the Middle East, soldiers would be supplied with their tropical uniforms; these would undergo some adaptations which, peculiarities apart, all too often resembled those of the men fighting on the opposite side of the front.

The Allies

British, Commonwealth and Imperial troops were supplied with a khaki drill service dress that included a jacket open at the collar (in the latest models) with four pockets, long trousers, boots and the ubiquitous tropical pith helmet. The khaki drill service dress was usually retained for use on the battlefield by officers, high-ranking ones in particular, while all others would use the simpler khaki drill shirt and short trousers on everyday duties. The drill shirt was a pullover made of Aertex, a light and very comfortable fabric, and had two breast pockets and removable shoulder straps. More often than not, the pith helmet was discarded in favour of the side caps, even the woollen European caps, or any other preferred headgear such as the Australian slouch, or bush hats, and the turban. Combat equipment included a steel helmet, model 1937

Axis Soldiers

The enemy that faced the British forces in 1941 was no longer the badly trained, and badly led, Italian soldiers of 1940. Apart from the Italian infantry divisions, still performing better than their counterpart in the early months of the war, all other units that fought in the Western Desert in 1941 were transferred from Europe. These included the Italian armoured and motorised infantry divisions, lacking battlefield experience and still under-trained, as well as the German units forming the Afrika Korps. Contrary to popular belief, they had not been trained or even prepared for desert or tropical warfare even though, unlike their Italian counterpart, they had combat experience. Since they mostly arrived in winter, neither the Italians nor the Germans had any real acclimatisation problems, which would start in the summer of 1941. Soon, sicknesses, mostly intestinal diseases, took a heavy toll on the Afrika Korps' soldiers, with an average loss of 22 per cent of its total strength between August and October 1941. These were the consequences of an inadequate diet, mostly made of canned meat (often Italian, made mostly of fat, cartilage and sinews), pulses, sausages, tuna and cheese while, owing to the inadequacy of the German field bakeries, long-life bread had to be supplied directly from Germany. Vitamins only came from lemons, and quantities varied considerably when the supply lanes across the Mediterranean were cut. Another factor was the lack of waistbands or corsets used to protect the belly, which only became compulsory in 1942.

13. A German tank crew. Note the black side cap of the European uniform and the boots worn by the soldier on the left.

14. *Australian 'diggers' arriving in Egypt. Apart from the typical slouch and bush hats, they largely used the pre-war uniform which was still worn during the Tobruk siege.*

webbing equipment made of belt, suspenders and ammunition pouches, and any other part of the equipment deemed necessary at that moment (such as haversack, gas mask containers, etc.), leather hobnailed 'ammunition' boots, along with woollen housetops worn with web anklets or short puttees, and any other ammunition carrier used for the weapon of the particular soldier. Finally, the canteen was essential in the heat of the desert and an item a soldier would never forget.

Certain items were not much appreciated, such as the 'Bombay bloomers', which were shorts with full turn-ups that could be folded, either up or down, but were found to be impractical. Others, like the regular shorts, saw limited use on the battlefield except in particular conditions, especially if fighting took place in rocky terrain or in winter temperatures. During the winter, European uniforms were preferred because they were more comfortable at night, although requiring the use of an overcoat, and were bearable during the daytime heat. British battledress, in its many variations (also including the New Zealand version) were therefore very popular and widely used during Operation Crusader.

Australians preferred their own pre-war woollen service dress, particularly in winter, which was made of a thigh-length tunic with four pockets and trousers fitted to their tan ankle boots with cloth gaiters; this combination was less aesthetically pleasing than the British battledress, but was much more practical.

The Axis

The Italians used a tropical version of their woollen European uniform, made from a lightweight fabric, but would often make use of the European grey-green woollen uniform during winter. Even if their tropical uniforms were well made and much appreciated, the Italians suffered greatly from a lack of suitable equipment, just having a small belt with a loop suspender (running around the neck rather than linking to the belt at the back), which could only carry limited weight, normally two ammunition pouches. The rest of their uniform was quite similar to the British version. The contrary can be said for the German uniform, specifically designed for use in Africa in 1940–41 using the old First World War German colonial uniforms. In 1941 the German soldiers would arrive in Libya fully dressed with a tropical pith helmet, a shirt with a necktie, a jacket (similar to the khaki drill service dress), breeches and long boots made of web and leather. The first item to be discarded was the necktie, followed soon by the breeches and the pith helmet. Boots were cut to the ankle, while straight, long trousers were used instead, and the peaked field cap was introduced. German equipment also included a webbing kit that, except for some leather details, did not differ much from the British version, apart from the widely used cylindrical, metal gas mask canister and the different ammunition pouches. Needless to say, civilian or civilian-style pieces of clothing like pullovers, 'cap comforters' or balaklava helmets, scarves, the British sleeved leather jerkin or any other piece of clothing could be purchased privately or taken from the enemy.

Given the climate and the terrain, clothing was an important factor in a soldier's everyday life, which was involved in two different fights: one against the enemy and the other one against the terrain and the elements. One of the peculiarities of the terrain in Cyrenaica, particularly along the coastline, was the practical impossibility for soldiers to dig deep trenches or even just foxholes for use as shelters, and all too often these were limited to shallow holes. This not only gave no protection against the cold at night, but also against the enemy (the use of piles of rocks, or 'sangars', was not recommended since these were easy to see and became a target at once). However, during the lull between battles, soldiers were much more concerned by the climate than anything else; dust and sand required frequent cleaning of the weapons, and everything else, while the intense heat (especially in summer), the swarms of flies, the insufficient diet and the scarcity of water could cause a range of ailments from sunburn to deep, infected sores and dysentery. Water was available in quantities; the average daily ration was about 5 litres per man, but since this included a variety of uses (cooking, washing and even for vehicles' radiators) the actual drinking ration was, generally speaking, down to about 1 litre per man per day. The situation was not any better in Tobruk, for the city lay on a salty water bed and water had to be brought in along with other supplies. Occasional events could make things even worse, with Ghibli (desert winds) and sandstorms the most destructive, as Major Hellmuth Frey (supply commander of the 15th Panzer Division) described in a letter home: 'The whole sky is brown-yellow for the dust. The sun only appears here and there. It's like the fog by us. But here it's burning hot. In the shade it's 44 degrees [Celsius]. The washing water I left in the canister was so hot, that I could barely wash myself.'[4] This, however, was only in April, and in early July he recorded a temperature of 75°C, 150km south of Tobruk. Rainstorms also occurred and, while certainly less annoying, they were hardly welcome, as Lieutenant Andrea Rebora of the Ariete Division wrote home on 18 November: 'My tent, like most of the others, was in a hole seventy to eighty

---

4   Frey, H., *Für Rommels Panzer durch die Wüste*, p. 31

centimetres deep. About half past eleven it starts raining: we think it's just a little shower that will not last for long and stay there easy, waiting for it to end. Rain starts to fall down by the bucket instead, and we are blocked where we were … Taking advantage of a pause I ran back to my tent to see if it still stood there. It did: half a metre outside the water, everything else completely flooded … bed, crates, table, boots, everything was under water … We rescue what we can … and put it out to dry … under the rain. Heavy rain started to fall again, it was soon dark … blankets, overcoats, jackets, everything was wet.'[5]

Combat added further strain, for supplies became uncertain (the Germans had strict orders not to wash when fighting), and there was also the threat of enemy attack. Most soldiers were armed with the standard rifle, not much different from those used by their fathers in the First World War. The British Short Magazine Lee Enfield, SMLE Mk III .303 (7.7mm), with its 'sword' bayonet, was roughly matched by the German 7.92mm Gewehr 98, although both the British and German rifles were heavier and more effective than the Italian standard 6.5mm Carcano 91 rifle. Squad and platoon leaders were often armed with sub-machine guns, or machine pistols, like the US-produced .45 Thompson 1928 (11.43mm, 600–700 rounds per minute) or the German 9mm MP 40 Schmeisser (450–540 rounds per minute). Light machine guns were the most typical support weapon; the British 7.7mm Mk II/III Bren gun could be fired on its integral bipod or mounted on a tripod, and had a 30-round magazine and a rate of fire of 450–550 rounds per minute. The Italian equivalent was the 6.5mm Breda 30 automatic rifle, with a 20-round magazine and a rate of fire of 400–500 rounds per minute. Heavy machine guns, like the British water-cooled .303 Vickers Mk I (500 rounds per minute) or the Italian air-cooled 8mm Breda model 37 and Fiat-Revelli model 35 (both 450 rounds per minute) provided, along with medium mortars (the British 3in, or 76mm, and the Italian and the German

5 Rebora, A., *Carri Ariete Combattono*, pp. 127–8

81mm), heavy fire support at company level. The Germans had a slight advantage with their 7.92mm MG 34, used either as a light (with its integral tripod) or heavy (mounted on a tripod) machine gun, firing at a rate of 800–900 rounds per minute.

The Tactics

It is a common misconception that the Western Desert was a theatre dominated exclusively by tank warfare, and Tobruk is a case in point. Infantry and artillery did play significant roles during the campaign, yet it is true that the role of armour was decisive in most of the cases. With its easily traversable and open spaces, many areas of the desert could be rapidly crossed by armoured and mechanised units that, striking at the rear of the enemy

15. Firing a water-cooled .303 Vickers heavy machine gun. Note the battledress and the use of leather jerkins; suitable clothing for the winter in Cyrenaica.

(such as at Beda Fomm), were often able to inflict considerable casualties. The German tactics, based on mobility and flexibility, were perfectly suited to this kind of warfare. Two key areas of German tactical superiority proved decisive when fighting in the open ground: their command system and their unit organisation.

The German command system was based on the 'mission command' style, whereby units (at every level) were not given specific orders but rather assigned a mission, leaving each individual commander with the details of how this was to be accomplished. They were also required to 'lead from the front', being as close as possible to the enemy to appreciate the situation first hand and react accordingly, which also accounts for the high casualty rate amongst German divisional commanders. The Panzer divisions were organised like miniature armies, including tank, infantry, artillery, reconnaissance and engineers units, which commanders would reorganise in an impromptu way on the battlefield by creating ad hoc Kampfgruppe, or battle groups, formed around one main unit with varying numbers of the other supporting formations. This way the Germans were able to achieve flexibility and speed of reaction, enabling them to concentrate their forces against enemy units and destroy them piecemeal.

These were factors the Eighth Army all too often lacked, as the British Army itself was rigidly structured on the 'top-down command' system, based on higher commanders issuing detailed and specific orders to their subordinates. This was further aggravated by other factors, specific to the early period of the Western Desert campaign; effective communication was essential for tactical flexibility, but the army suffered from both a lack of suitable equipment and lousy radio communication procedures, which often allowed the Germans to intercept British orders easily. The lack of modern and reliable radio sets would create many problems for the Eighth Army during Operation Crusader, particularly when its command and communication virtually collapsed during the first week; 4th Armoured Brigade's loss of four radio sets on 22 November 1941 left the entire unit practically without command, or even control from higher headquarters, during the entire day. The other factor was the large collection of units from different countries which formed the Eighth Army; although they all shared similar structures and organisations, all based on the British Army model, there was (particularly in the first years) a keen attitude of having the British armoured units 'leading the battle', leaving the Commonwealth and Imperial forces to provide support. Not to be forgotten or underrated is the effect that the early, easy victories over the Italians had on the British forces; the first meeting with the Germans (and even the meeting with other Italian units) would prove how the sense of superiority achieved during O'Connor's offensive had to be regained in some other way on the battlefield.

Another basic problem was inter-arms co-operation, which greatly influenced the course of Operation Compass. Most British commanders advocated 'pure' armoured warfare, with tank versus tank combat, although this belief was shattered when the Germans used a combination of tanks and anti-tank guns to devastating effect. Experiments were made with 'battle group' style formations, the 'Jock columns', which were usually composed of a mixture of infantry, artillery, engineers, anti-tank and aircraft guns. However, their small sizes (the units forming them usually varied from company to platoon size) made them no match for the German Kampfgruppe.

Tanks and anti-tank guns played a major role during the campaign, particularly in Operation Compass, and it is worth

JOCK COLUMNS

Named after Lieutenant Colonel 'Jock' Campbell of the 4th Royal Horse Artillery who pioneered them, these small and very mobile groups were first used against the Italians in 1940. They were used to confuse enemy reconnaissance and harass the enemy rear lines, which they did effectively in November 1941.

noting that the British tanks started to lose the edge over enemy tanks at this stage of the war. In 1940–41 the British light Mk VI, Cruiser A9 and A10 tanks (Cruiser Mk I and II) were not decisively superior to the Italian medium tanks, lacking mechanical reliability, armour (14–30mm maximum), speed (25kph) and gunnery, with the 2-pounder (40mm) gun providing the basic British tank and anti-tank gun until El Alamein. This edge was eventually regained by the Mk II Matilda infantry tank, which, with its 78mm armour, could only be penetrated by the fearsome German 88mm Flak (anti-aircraft) gun. The new A13 and A15 Crusader tank still suffered from poor reliability and weaponry, even though the armour (up to 40mm) and speed (up to 44kph) did improve. The Mk III Valentine infantry tank did not differ much from the Matilda, being itself armed with the 2-pounder gun, while an improvement came with the US-built M3 Stuart light tank, armed with a 37mm gun, up to 51mm of armour and a top speed of about 60kph; its reliability and easiness to drive earned it the name 'Honey' from British tank crews.

The real problem with British tanks was the 2-pounder gun, as although it could penetrate the frontal armour of both the

16. A German 88mm Flak gun being towed. This was the most feared weapon in the German inventory, but was only available in small numbers.

German and Italian tanks, there were no high-explosive rounds for it and was therefore quite ineffective against the German anti-tank guns. These were the real danger for the British tanks; the German tank inventory in 1941 had only seen limited improvements from the pre-war years, with both the Panzer I and II equipped with a 20mm main gun and a machine gun, roughly equalling the Mk VI, while both the Panzer III (the main German battle tank) and IV medium tanks were both lightweight, had good speed (up to 40kph) and excellent reliability, but also lacked armour (up to 35–37mm) and gunnery. The Panzer III also had a 50mm and the Panzer IV a 75mm short-barrelled gun, mostly effective when firing high-explosive rounds. In essence, the German Panzer and the British Cruiser tanks were similar in capability, able to penetrate each other's armoured plates at a medium distance of about 500–800m. The later infantry tanks were more of a problem for the Germans since they could resist German Panzers' shells up to a range of 100m or less.

Basically, the Germans enjoyed two distinct advantages: their speed and manoeuvrability (superior to that of the British infantry tanks) enabled them to outflank the British tanks, while the superior German anti-tank guns were able to deal with them at great distance. In 1941 the Germans were equipped with, apart from the outdated 37mm gun, the standard 50mm anti-tank gun, which was able to deal with the Cruiser tanks at long range (500–1,000m), and the infantry tanks at close range, with its high rate of fire (10–15 rounds per minute). However, the 88mm Flak gun – also used in an anti-tank role – was the real nightmare for British tank crews as it could engage and destroy not only the Cruiser, but also the infantry tanks at a range of 2,000m or more. It must be said, though, that it was never available in large numbers and was rather easy to see given its high silhouette, even if this may have served as both an advantage and a disadvantage for the British tank crews that faced it.

GERMAN ANTI-AIRCRAFT

The German Flak *(Flieger Abwehr Kanone)*, or anti-aircraft, units were equipped with the fearsome dual-purpose 88mm gun and wreaked havoc upon British tank crews. The first unit to arrive in Libya was the 1st Battalion of the 33rd Flak Regiment, part of the 5th Light Division, in February 1941.

17. *A German 50mm PAK 38 (*Panzer Abwehr Kanone*) anti-tank gun. A very effective weapon, but not available in large numbers to the Afrika Korps in 1941. Note the tropical pith hat worn by the crew, soon to be discharged.*

THE DAYS
BEFORE BATTLE

The Terrain

Cyrenaica is one of those places which prove the old saying, 'Geography dictates history'. The region, stretching from El Agheila in the west to Sollum in the east, is characterised by the large bulge east of the Gulf of Sirte. It is dominated by the Jebel Akhdar, the 'green mountains', and stretches out into the sea from Benghazi to the Gulf of Bomba, just to the west of Gazala. As the Italians experienced first hand in February 1941, a modern mechanised army can cross the desert from El Mechili to Msus, and from there move either to the coast or further west to Agedabia relatively easily and at fast speed, turning the whole area between Derna and Benghazi into a deathtrap. This factor determined the importance of the three main harbours in Cyrenaica: Benghazi (the largest), Tobruk and Bardia (the smallest). Benghazi was ruled out as a main supply centre because it was too exposed to enemy attack and too far away from the frontier; Bardia, too, was of little use because of its small size and proximity to the frontier. That made Tobruk the only available supply centre, as it was relatively easy to defend and close enough to the frontier to support any advance into Egypt.

The Western Desert has been described many times as the ideal battle arena, without the major hurdles and hindrances one would find in Europe, including a civilian population; however, this is only partly true for there was a civilian population in Cyrenaica, including some 100,000 Italian settlers and a large number of Arabs, some of which belonged to the Senussi tribes that fought against the Italians and the British during the First World War. Even the battle arena was not void of hurdles and hindrances, as the 'green mountains', like a good deal of the coastal strip west of Tobruk, enjoyed a temperate climate and a terrain not much different from Tunisia or southern Italy, but further to the south or east, into the desert, the greater the climate and terrain changes. In fact, the actual battles took place in a rather narrow 100km strip of land between the sea and the desert, in the area between El Gazala and the Libyan–Egyptian frontier, which if still not the real Sahara (the sand sea is further south), was at least desert enough for those who fought there.

The desert area was not entirely made of sand, but also of rocky terrain more suitable for vehicles. Even though tracked vehicles could move almost at will, the wheeled vehicles were mostly bound to the paved road, such as the 'via Balbia' which ran along the coast, or to the tracks (*trigh* in Arabic) which ran over suitable ground. These tracks caused problems for wheeled vehicles since they were unmarked (only the most important ones had barrels put along the path) and, after a while, the tyre marks of previous vehicles either disappeared or led outside the tracks, with the risk of leading other vehicles into deeper sand. Closer to the sea, the terrain featured another impassable obstacle: the dried river beds, known as wadi, which formed rocky escarpments running almost parallel to the sea. The biggest group of these stretches from Bardia to Tobruk, some 20–25km south of the coast, with a depth of 8km and an average height of about 60m. The Halfaya Pass, or 'Hellfire Pass' in colloquial English, was a key position since it crossed these escarpments on the via Balbia coastal road. The largest group runs to the south and west of Tobruk, in the areas of Sidi Rezegh and Ed Duda, deemed suitable to leaguer troops (establish a provisional camp) and keep them hidden from aerial reconnaissance. The Tobruk area was itself largely dominated by broken, rocky terrain

18. A British dugout overlooking the Halfaya Pass. Note the interesting mixture of uniforms and the overcoats, a necessity once the sun had set.

and alternating dunes ranging from 30–60m high, with the desert taking over from the steppe some 30–40km inland.

Movement was not only hindered at times, but also rendered very dangerous; vehicles moving in the desert would raise sand and dust, which made them easily detectable from the air and a possible target for enemy (or even friendly) aircraft and artillery fire. This was quite a common problem, but it mainly afflicted the Germans as they were unused to the terrain and lacked proper training. Weather also had an influence, as the temperatures in summer can reach in excess of 55°C by midday, which made any activity almost impossible. The situation was much better in winter, with an average of 25°C, but temperatures would drop dramatically shortly after sunset, and on occasions below zero. The Ghibli, or desert wind, also raised heavy sandstorms and made any kind of movement impossible, and since the movement of many vehicles in a small area raised huge quantities of dust and sand, the number and intensity of the sandstorms increased significantly. Sandstorms could often hide units while moving, but in some cases they caused a loss of orientation which can prove fatal when travelling in the desert. Rainfalls are quite rare in the area of Tobruk, with the bulk falling in the aptly named 'green mountains' at an average of 624mm per year, but even in the Tobruk area there were occasional rainfalls at an average of 50–100mm per year. The problem was that all too often these were the result of large, tropical rainstorms which caused flooding, and was uncomfortable and even dangerous for those who had chosen a wadi to set up camp.

Tobruk: The Early Attacks

In the evening of 8 April Rommel ordered his forces to press on with the attacks toward Tmimi and Tobruk. For this purpose he formed another Kampfgruppe under the command of General Prittwitz, 15th Panzer Division commander, which was made of the mobile units of the 5th Light Division. The following day they approached Tobruk, reporting the presence of a large number of ships in the harbour and that the enemy had already withdrawn into the fortress. Rommel reacted immediately to the news and ordered Prittwitz's group to move south-east of Tobruk, while the group led by General Streich moved to the south-west, and the Brescia Division advanced along the coast to the east. The aim was to take Tobruk with a *coup de main* using the German Kampfgruppe, both attacking from the south-east. In Rommel's view this would not be a difficult task, as ships in Tobruk harbour suggested an evacuation was already under way, and Rommel thought it was necessary to attack the fortress as soon as possible before some sort of defence could be organised. The situation looked so bright that Rommel revealed his aims; on 10 April he stated that the enemy was giving way to the Axis forces and therefore he wanted to prevent any escape from Tobruk (including any breakout attempt) in order to destroy what was left of the enemy forces. Once this aim was achieved, his Afrika Korps could resume the advance to its primary goal: the Suez Canal.

With the 9th Australian Division and other units withdrawing into the fortress, General Wavell flew to Tobruk on 8 April, along with

WAR IN THE SAHARA

The seizure of the oasis of Kufra and Jarabub early in 1941 marked the beginning of the war fought in the Libyan sand sea, the Sahara. To face the enemy threat the Italians strengthened their forces in the area (under the Libyan Sahara Command) to some 4,000 Italian and Libyan troops by January 1942.

19. An Australian sentry is watching Tobruk harbour, the only way in which reinforcements and supplies could reach the beleaguered garrison.

the 7th Australian Division commander, General John Lavarack, who was to take command. Two days later, with the last Australian units moving into the already surrounded fortress, new arrangements were made: Lavarack went back to his division and General Leslie Morshead, 9th Australian Division's commander, took over command of Tobruk. The bulk of the defenders were made of the 9th Australian Division and its three brigades (20th, 24th and 26th), plus the 18th Brigade of the 7th Australian Division and a mixture of British and Indian troops. Overall strength included 14,270 Australians, 9,000

British and some 5,700 mixed British, Australian and Indian troops, plus 3,000 Libyan labourers. Lavarack, and later Morshead, decided to defend the outer perimeter of the Italian fortress, which was 54km long, stretching out from the coast for an average of 15km and with an arc 45km wide. Morshead quickly decided how the defence was to be structured: the perimeter was to be defended by the three brigades of the 9th Australian Division (from left to right: 26th, 20th and 24th), each one supported by a regiment of field guns. Their task was to hold their ground, to dominate no-man's-land by undertaking night patrols and, in the meantime, to organise the defences in depth and to create a mobile reserve.

The defences of the Tobruk line were quite impressive, although this did not prevent its seizure in early January. The terrain closest to the coast was more favourable for the defence than the southern bend, but the entire perimeter – surrounded by an incomplete line of anti-tank ditches and barbed wire – was made of a series of strongpoints at 700m intervals, both on the front line and in depth. Each strongpoint included three 'Tobruk' bunkers connected by a trench and protected with sandbagged parapets, and each had a ditch around them which was often booby-trapped and, sometimes, heavily mined. Another defence line was built closer to Tobruk, while Australian 'diggers' started to improve the defences that had either been smashed by their own comrades a few months before or had simply deteriorated through neglect. Effective as it was against infantry, the line was not so much of a hindrance for armour, but, luckily, tanks and anti-tank guns were not in short supply; 3rd Armoured Brigade grouped all the tank units within the Tobruk fortress and, along with the 1st and 4th RTR, had a total of sixty tanks in running order (including four Matilda, twenty-three Cruiser and thirty-three light tanks), plus another twenty-six were under repair. Also available were 113 anti-tank guns; half were captured Italian 32mm and 47mm guns, and the other half were British 2-pounders. The Germans, who only had Italian maps (often inaccurate) weeks later, were unaware of the extent of the fortifications at Tobruk and of the actual forces that were defending them.

Early in the morning of 10 April Rommel reached Prittwitz and ordered him to attack Tobruk immediately along the coastal road. Prittwitz moved the German 8th Machine Gun Battalion forward, followed by the Brescia Division, and reached the fortified line at about 9 a.m., only to face British armoured cars blocking the road. The German column, led by Prittwitz, then swung south and tried to reach the higher ground at Ras el Medauar, but soon fell under fire from concealed Australian positions. Eventually the column withdrew after General Prittwitz had been killed, and Rommel subsequently ordered the 3rd Reconnaissance Battalion to advance west toward Bardia. Rommel then moved the Brescia Division to the west of Tobruk and deployed a battle group to the south, which consisted of the 8th Machine Gun Battalion and twenty-five Panzers from the 5th Panzer Regiment, plus ten anti-tank guns. The group attacked Tobruk on 11 April, moving along the road from El Adem before running into anti-tank ditches and Australian anti-tank fire, losing one German and two Italian tanks and eventually withdrawing after only half an hour. The following day the 3rd Reconnaissance Battalion seized Bardia, while the rebuilt Western Desert Force had already withdrawn east of the Libyan–Egyptian frontier.

Rommel attempted to maintain the pace of the advance, but after an attack on 12 April by the 5th Panzer Regiment on the Tobruk defences to the east, the advance slowed before approaching the Allied front line; the German forces prepared

TOBRUK BUNKERS

The Tobruk bunkers were made of a concrete underground shelter for taking cover under enemy fire, and of an outer, unprotected ring used for returning fire. Although the ring did not have a gun cupola and could only be used by small groups, it had the advantage of being hard to spot and directly fire upon.

20. General Leslie Morshead talking to one of his brigadiers. Morshead was the commander of 9th Australian Division and as such also commander of the besieged Tobruk garrison.

a major attack for the following day. Again moving along the El Adem road, the 8th Machine Gun Battalion, supported by the 200th Engineer Battalion, attacked the positions held by the Australian 2/17 Battalion at sunset on 13 April. After vicious fighting at close range, the German soldiers managed to open a gap behind one of the strongpoints and at 4 a.m. on 14 April the Panzers of the 5th Panzer Regiment broke through the defence lines and advanced toward 'King's Cross', the road junction of the El Adem road and the via Balbia. At daylight they were met with fire from three anti-tank battalions and one 25-pounder field gun battalion and, lacking infantry support (held up by Australian fire, which had also killed the commander of the 8th Machine Gun Battalion), they were forced to withdraw at 7.30 a.m. One

TOBRUK'S VC

During a counterattack led by the 2nd/17th Battalion on 13–14 April, Corporal Jack Edmondson was seriously wounded by enemy machine-gun fire; nevertheless, he continued to attack the enemy and fought magnificently, only to die the morning after. His VC was the first awarded to an Australian in the Second World War.

hour later the battle was over; the 5th Panzer Regiment had lost seventeen tanks and the 8th Machine Gun Battalion had suffered 280 casualties. Other attacks did follow, but all were unsuccessful. On 16 April the Italian Ariete and Trento divisions attacked at Ras el Medauar, but were soon forced to withdraw. The following day Rommel personally led an attack on the same position with Italian units supported by two German infantry companies, but again to no avail. At this point he was forced to realise that rest, refitting and reinforcements were needed before his forces could attempt to break through the Tobruk defence line once again.

Tobruk: The Siege

After a week the situation was clear: Tobruk was not going to be evacuated and the British were not going to give way to Rommel's advance. However, an Axis advance toward Egypt was not possible until Tobruk had been seized, given the lack of forces and supplies plaguing the beleaguered troops. The only solution was a major attack to break through the defence line and seize Tobruk, something made possible thanks to the arrival of the first units of the 15th Panzer Division in April. Not everything went smoothly, however; on 27 April the chief of operations at the German army staff, General Friedrich Paulus (later defeated at Stalingrad), arrived in Libya to evaluate the situation at first hand, which in his estimate was critical given

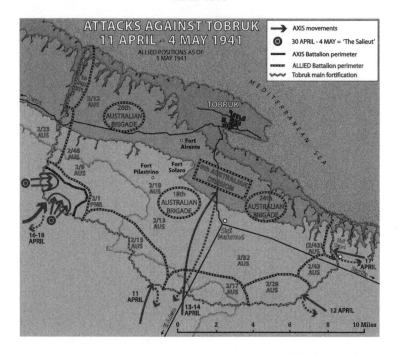

the supply problems and the lack of forces. Initially he would not authorise Rommel to take troops from the Libyan–Egyptian frontier to attack Tobruk, but eventually agreed on 29 April, after the Italians had given the green light.

The attack was to take place in the area of Ras el Medauar, and this time at full strength. The northern shoulder was made of Kampfgruppe Holtzendorff, with three infantry, one engineer, one anti-tank and one artillery battalion from the 15th Panzer Divison; the southern flank was formed from Kampfgruppe Kirchheim of the 5th Light Division, with one infantry, one engineer, two anti-tank and one artillery battalion, plus one Panzer battalion. Troops of the 15th Panzer Division were inexperienced in desert warfare and also had been without proper food rations in the last days leading up to the attack. Rommel forbade any reconnaissance of the ground to prevent alerting the enemy (an order General Kirchheim disobeyed), but this was unnecessary as the Australians immediately detected the German build-up. The attack started at 6.15 p.m., hitting the positions of the Australian 2/24 Battalion, and soon the German assault troops had managed to infiltrate the Australian strongpoints and began to eliminate them one by one. Kirchheim's battle group made the most initial progress, and Corporal Bob McLeish describes why this time the German attack had more success: 'Their machine guns kept our heads down and their cannon blasted away our sandbag parapet. The sand got into our MGs and we spent as much time cleaning them as we did firing them, but we sniped at the infantry whenever we got the chance ... We threw hand grenades at them [the Panzers] but these bounced off, and the best we could do was to keep the infantry from getting closer than a hundred yards.'[6]

As night fell the situation became confused; troops of the 15th Panzer Division lost their orientation and moved to the wrong positions, with the result that the Australian strongpoint at Ras el Medauar was left intact, leaving a gap between the two German assault groups. While their strongpoints were being taken one by one, General Morshead and his Australian units faced a critical moment, but were left in the dark because telephone lines had been cut by an artillery barrage. By midnight it was clear that the Germans had penetrated deeply into the defence line, although parts continued to resist. Morshead ordered the mobilisation of the Matilda tanks of 7th RTR and, with the 18th Australian Brigade, was put in readiness for a counterattack. Dawn on 1 May brought thick fog across the battlefield, and Rommel faced a difficult situation; Paulus remarked that the attack could not be successful without fresh units and ammunition supplies, while the remaining Australian strongpoint between the two attacking groups was a major hurdle to an infantry advance. At 8 a.m. the 5th Panzer Regiment attacked across the German bridgeheads

---

6 Lyman, *Siege*, p. 173

21. A patrol crossing the wire around Tobruk. Active defence, which included patrols and raids, was essential to Morshead's defence of the fortress.

with all its available tanks, which totalled seventy-nine, including the light ones. They split into two groups and advanced beyond the German front line, but were soon to discover that the infantry had not been able to follow them; Australian anti-tank battalions held their fire until the last moment, before opening up on the Panzers as they entered a minefield. Events are told by an unknown Panzer officer: 'The English artillery fires on us at once. We attack. No German patrol goes in front to reconnoitre. Tier upon tier of guns boom out from the triangular fortification

22. A 20mm Breda anti-aircraft gun in a sandbagged pit. Mainly intended for use against aircraft, it was also used against the AFVs, although not very effective against tanks

before us. The two light troops of the company and my left section are detailed off to make a flanking movement. I attack. Wireless message: "Commander of 6 Coy, hit on track". Then things happen suddenly … A frightful crash in front and to the right. Direct hit from artillery shell. No! It must be a mine … 5 metres back – new detonation. Mine underneath to the left … Wireless message: "Getting back went on mine again."'[7]

Two hours later they withdrew, leaving behind fourteen tanks. The Germans then started to secure the area and widen the breach, making progress on the northern shoulder. Morshead decided to counterattack, with the result that two British Cruiser and four Matilda tanks were lost. The loss of the Matilda tanks stalled the counterattack, while the infantry faced heavy

---

7 Forty, G., *Afrika Korps at War 1*, p. 113

opposition; the 2/48 Australian Battalion was repulsed 250m short of its objective and suffered heavy casualties. On 2 May the Germans consolidated the bridgehead and the 18th Australian Brigade counterattacked again, retaking one strongpoint before disorganisation and heavy German fire eventually repelled the attack and the brigade withdrew with 150 casualties. During these three days the Germans lost more than 1,200 men, advanced only 3km into the defence line and were now facing three Australian battalions. General Paulus, before leaving Libya on 7 May, gave Rommel an army staff directive that imposed a delay on the decisive attacks against Tobruk until reinforcements were available. Paulus remarked that the problem in Africa was neither Tobruk nor Sollum, but supply.

The battle of Ras el Medauar marked the beginning of the siege, which involved air attacks against the city, its harbour and the Australian positions, artillery bombardments, patrols and harassing attacks from both sides. That did not stop work for the 'diggers', and two more defence lines were built in the months that followed. Strongpoints on the outer defence line were improved and new minefields were laid, often by removing the mines laid by the Axis forces and placing them somewhere else. Daily life was characterised by a lack of water (tea was made with sea water), flies and dust, with the Ghibli bringing up more dust at least once every four days. Hot meals were available for those at the front line, but only at night, and apart from those close to the sea, where a hand grenade could be used for fishing, all others had to do with the ubiquitous bully beef. All this while under constant shelling from the Axis artillery. It was a hard life, and intense fighting continued on a small scale, yet no real hate was to divide the men on the two sides of the front, rather more a mutual respect, as reported by a German battalion commander: 'The Australians … are extraordinarily tough fighters. The German is more active in the attack but the enemy stakes his life in the defence and fights to the last and with extreme cunning. Our men, usually easygoing and unsuspecting, fall easily

23. Lack of suitable artillery support was one of the main reasons of concern for General Morshead during the siege. At Tobruk captured artillery guns were often used.

RATS AND SOLDIERS

The Australian defenders of Tobruk proudly acquired the name of 'rats of Tobruk' after Lord Haw-Haw, the British commentator on German propaganda radio, said they were 'caught in a trap like rats'. That must not be confused with the name 'Desert Rats', which was taken by the 7th Armoured Division after it adopted the Jerboa as its divisional emblem.

into his traps. Enemy snipers have astounding results ... Several NCOs [non-commissioned officers] of the battalion have been shot through the head with the first shot while making observations in the front line.'[8]

On 19 August the Australian troops were relieved at Tobruk, and were replaced by the British 70th Division and the Polish Brigade.

8 Lyman, *Siege*, p. 180

The relief went often – but not always – smoothly, with the last stage (lasting from 12–15 October) managing to bring 7,138 men into the harbour and take 7,234 men out, plus 727 wounded, with each single ship being unloaded and loaded in no more than thirty minutes to leave the harbour before daylight. Between March and December 1941 the total losses suffered by the troops in Tobruk had been 832 killed, 2,177 wounded and 941 prisoners, with the 9th Australian Division alone suffering 749 killed, 1,996 wounded and 604 prisoners between April and October. As the Australian journalist Alan Moorehead wrote, 'They were the Rats of Tobruk … They wanted to fight. They were delighted to be in the desert.'[9] And they would be back.

Battles at the Frontier: Operations Brevity and Battleaxe

On 12 May the 'Tiger' convoy reached Alexandria after crossing the Mediterranean, bringing much-needed reinforcements from Britain, particularly tanks (including eighty-two Cruiser and 135 infantry) and aircraft. Before these were distributed to the troops, Operation Brevity was started at the Libyan–Egyptian frontier on 15 May. The German advance into Cyrenaica and the successes in the Balkans brought significant changes to the situation, as did the news of the arrival of a second German division in Libya. The plan for Brevity envisaged an encounter battle, with the British forces supported from the air while advancing along three parallel routes toward the Axis positions in the Sidi Omar–Halfaya Pass area. To the left the 7th Armoured Brigade Group (with twenty-nine Cruiser tanks and three columns of the support group) was to outflank the enemy position east of Sidi Omar from the desert and reach Sidi Azeiz to the south-west of Bardia. At the centre, 22nd Guards Brigade Group (twenty-four infantry tanks) was to attack the Halfaya Pass from the west and advance to Fort

---

9   Quoted in: Bungay, S., *Alamein*, p. 88

Capuzzo, while on the left the 2nd Rifle Brigade was to attack Halfaya and Sollum in an advance along the coast.

Early operations on 15 May were quite successful, with the 22nd Guards Brigade quickly seizing the Halfaya Pass, albeit at the cost of seven tanks, before advancing to Capuzzo. The weak Axis units defending the area, the equivalent of one German and one Italian battalion with anti-tank guns and reconnaissance units, had been reinforced by a Panzer battalion on 8 May after German intelligence reported that an enemy attack was imminent. The 22nd Guards Brigade seized Capuzzo, but again tank losses, nine infantry tanks, prevented any further exploitation north. At this point the Panzer battalion counterattacked the British positions at Capuzzo, eventually compelling the 22nd Guards Brigade to withdraw after heavy losses. The threat posed by the 7th Armoured Brigade was then dealt with by a Panzer battalion from the 5th Panzer Regiment and a newly arrived battalion from the 8th Panzer Regiment of the 15th Panzer Division. Both units chased the withdrawing 7th Brigade and eventually, on 16 May, the Germans halted on the Sidi Omar–Sollum line, retaking Halfaya from

24. *Matilda tanks on the move. During Operation Crusader the British 1st Army Tank Brigade, supporting the XIII Corps, and the 32nd Armoured Brigade were equipped with Matilda tanks at Tobruk.*

the British. Tank losses for the British were severe: five infantry tanks lost and sixteen damaged against the loss of three German Panzers.

Operation Battleaxe was Wavell's first attempt to relieve Tobruk and restore the situation in Libya. First drafted on 1 May, he finally gave the orders for the plan on 28 May; its aim was to defeat the enemy in the frontier area, then to advance north to Bardia where a major attack was to be launched toward the Tobruk–El Adem area. Afterwards, British forces were to exploit and advance toward Derna and El Mechili. Units on both sides were reorganised; the Germans had the 5th Light Division along with the newly arrived 15th Panzer Division, while on the British side was the 7th Armoured Division. Along with it, and aiming to strike on the left flank in open desert, was the 4th Indian Division (partly engaged in Syria and partly being transported from East Africa), plus the 4th Armoured Brigade, which was to advance along the coast up to Bardia. Both sides had roughly 200 tanks at their disposal and about the same numbers in terms of infantry, but a crucial factor was the decision by General Beresford-Peirse to place his HQ at Sidi Barrani, about 100km away from the battlefield.

On 15 June the British attack started, but the Germans were fully prepared for it. Early operations were not promising as fifteen out of eighteen infantry tanks were lost at Halfaya due to 88mm Flak guns, while German anti-tank guns took a heavy toll on the advancing 7th Armoured Division west of Sollum. Nevertheless, the British advance overran the German artillery and threatened Fort Capuzzo, which compelled the 8th Panzer Regiment to counterattack. It could not prevent the 7th Armoured Division from seizing Capuzzo, but during the night it was joined by the 5th Panzer Regiment led by Rommel, and a hastily prepared defence line was established south of Bardia. However, thanks to the exploitation of careless British radio communications by German intelligence, Rommel had a clear picture of the situation and prepared for his next move. Early on 16 June the 8th Panzer Regiment attacked the positions of the 7th Armoured Division west of Capuzzo and, although the attack was unsuccessful,

25. German officers inspecting a destroyed Matilda infantry tank. The loss of four of these at Tobruk on 2 May 1941 was a shock for the British.

it prevented the 4th Armoured Brigade from being able to join up with the 4th Indian Division in a renewed attack against the Halfaya Pass. This enabled the German tank commanders to join the 5th and 8th Panzer regiments together and attack to the west, outflanking the 7th Armoured Division and chasing it back to the frontier while the infantry overran Sidi Omar. Even though the Germans did not prevail, at the end of the day the two British regiments were left with only twenty-one tanks fit for combat.

Rommel's attack came early on 17 June, with both Panzer regiments striking from the frontier toward Halfaya and to the rear of the British positions at Capuzzo, catching the 4th Armoured Brigade out in the open. The 22nd Guards Brigade's positions were also threatened from the south, and with only a few tanks in running order available (twenty-two Cruiser and seventeen infantry tanks) and given the faulty radio communications which prevented any control over units on the battlefield, Wavell had to make a decision. He flew to join 7th Armoured Division HQ and arrived at 11.45 a.m. along with Beresford-Peirse, only to find that the divisional commander, General Messervy, had already ordered

THE DESERT FOX

Rommel started to become a respected figure amongst the
British soldiers following Operation Battleaxe, when they
started to call him 'the Desert Fox'. The name was used for
the first time in the United Kingdom early in
1942, and later by German propaganda.

a withdrawal in the view that this was the only way to extricate
the 22nd Guards Brigade from its current positions. Wavell at first
wanted to cancel the order and to issue his own to counterattack,
but the actual situation eventually suggested that Messervy's
withdrawal order was correct, and at nightfall the spearheads
of the Western Desert Force retreated to the Sidi Barrani area.
Operation Battleaxe thus ended with British forces having lost 122
killed, 588 wounded and 259 missing, plus twenty-seven Cruiser
tanks (out of the original ninety) and sixty-four infantry tanks (out
of about 100). German losses amounted to ninety-three killed,
350 wounded and 235 missing (Italians casualties included 586
killed and missing, 691 wounded), and only five light and seven
medium Panzers were put out of action. The Desert Fox had won
his battle, and a few days later Wavell was replaced by General
Claude Auchinleck at the head of Middle East Command.

Operation Crusader: The Planning and the Opposing Forces

Operation Battleaxe was followed by a lull and a period of
uncertainty, as neither side had enough strength for another
offensive, and both sides began to rest, refit and reorganise their
units. The summer brought news of the German invasion of the
Soviet Union, and the autumn was to become a period of planning.
Early in September, Auchinleck instructed the commander of the
Eighth Army, General Cunningham, to study a plan for an offensive

aimed at delivering a direct thrust toward Tobruk. The plan was a scaled-up version of Battleaxe, just as that plan had been a scaled-up version of Brevity. The right wing of the offensive was to attack the enemy positions along the frontier and at Bardia, while the main thrust, or the left wing, was to advance into the desert and outflank the enemy positions to bring the German armour into battle and destroy it. Subsequently, a breakout from Tobruk and the two-pronged advance from the south were to relieve the fortress and compel the enemy to withdraw to the west. Even though the German Panzers were seen as the real objective of the offensive, since without their defeat any further progress would have been impossible, there was not much thought given to how they should be destroyed in the open, apart from simply relying upon superior British fighting qualities. The XIII Corps, including the 4th Indian and the New Zealand divisions, was given the task of attacking the enemy on the frontier along the Sidi Omar–Halfaya line, partly to be outflanked, and to advance to Bardia.

The newly formed XXX Corps was to move from Egypt and advance on a broad front some 50–100km deep into the desert from the coastline, aiming at the Trigh El Abd (the track running from Bir Hakeim to Bir El Gubi and to the south of the Sidi Omar) and meeting, according to the forecast, the German Panzers somewhere around Gabr Saleh, south-east of Sidi Rezegh. The bulk of XXX Corps was made up of the 7th Armoured

26. General Sir Alan Cunningham, the first commander of the Eighth Army, formed on 18 September 1941.

Division, now reorganised with the 7th and 22nd Armoured brigades comprising most of the available Cruiser tanks. The 7th Armoured Brigade had eighty-eight of the early A13 Cruiser tanks, plus fifty-three of the new A15 Crusader tanks for a total of 141 tanks, while the 22nd Armoured Brigade had 155 A15 Crusader tanks. The 4th Armoured Brigade Group, attached to the division, added 165 new M3 Stuart tanks along with one infantry and one artillery battalion, while the divisional support group added one anti-tank, two artillery and two infantry battalions. All in all, the XXX Corps had 477 tanks (173 Stuart and 304 Cruiser), while the 1st Army Tank Brigade, supporting the XIII Corps, added three more Cruiser and 132 infantry tanks, about half Matilda and half Valentine types, and the British 32nd Army Tank Brigade in Tobruk also had thirty-two Cruiser, twenty-five light and sixty-nine Matilda tanks. The overall strength of the Eighth Army was 118,000 troops, supported by 530 aircraft and with an immense quantity of supplies carefully deployed in supply dumps in various areas behind the frontier. Worth noting is that almost the entire Eighth Army was now fully motorised, essential for conducting desert warfare.

The balance of forces was almost entirely against Rommel, for he had at his disposal only 249 tanks in his two Panzer divisions, seventy of which were light tanks. The overall strength of the Afrika Korps was 48,500, but this included about 11,000 who were suffering from bad (or complete lack of) acclimatisation.

OPERATION FLIPPER

The mission was undertaken by a party of the No. 11 (Scottish) Commando unit led by Colonel Geoffrey Keyes. Landed on the night of 16/17 November 1941 by submarine near Apollonia (west of Derna), they attempted to attack enemy command centres, including Rommel's presumed HQ. However, the mission failed and only two of the group made their way back.

27. British Mk VI Crusader Cruiser tanks (A15), equipping both the 7th and 22nd Armoured brigades during Operation Crusader.

FIRST SAS OPERATION

On the night of 16/17 November 1941 the 'L' Detachment of the 1st Special Service Brigade (later the SAS), led by Captain David Sterling, was airdropped in the Gazala-Tmimi area and tasked with attacking enemy airfields. The party of fifty-seven was dropped too far south of the target and the mission had to be cancelled.

The Italian forces added to these figures for a total of 100,000 more troops, 54,000 of which were combat units at the front (mostly lacking, partly or completely, motor transport). However, the two mobile divisions, part of the Corpo d'Armata di Manovra (CAM, the armoured Ariete and the motorised Trieste), were only 17,000 strong and had 160 medium tanks, without taking into account the almost useless light 'tankettes'. The Axis forces could also call on 140 German and 200 Italian aircraft for support. The fact is that Rommel could fight a battle, but he was greatly hampered by two factors: the first was the lack of supplies, which would have worsened during the battle, and the second was that he neither expected nor was prepared for a British offensive at the time; his attention was almost exclusively focused on a plan for the renewed attack against Tobruk. He would soon be forced to change his mind.

THE BATTLEFIELD:
WHAT ACTUALLY HAPPENED?

The Opening Moves (18–20 November)

18 November	Start of Operation Crusader, the winter battle in the Western Desert. British forces advance deep into Cyrenaica
19 November	British 22nd Armoured Brigade clashes with the Italian Ariete Division at Bir el Gubi and suffers heavy losses. British 7th Armoured Brigade seizes Sidi Rezegh
20 November	British 7th Armoured Brigade clashes with German and Italian forces at Sidi Rezegh, while the 4th Armoured Brigade suffers heavy losses in its encounter with the Afrika Korps at Gabr Saleh

At dawn on 18 November, after a three-day postponement imposed by the delayed arrival of the 22nd Armoured Brigade, Operation Crusader started with Eighth Army units and formations moving from their jumping-off positions in the Egyptian desert and advancing deep into eastern Cyrenaica. The first day of the advance was quite uneventful, but not without problems; leading reconnaissance armoured cars occasionally met with their German counterpart, who reported back about the British advance. Bad

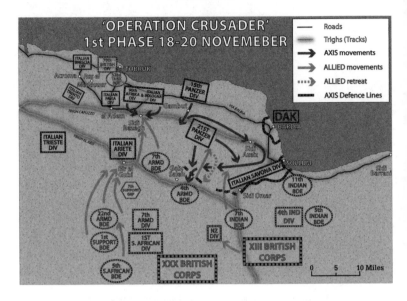

'OPERATION CRUSADER'
1st PHASE 18-20 NOVEMEBER

Roads
Trighs (Tracks)
AXIS movements
ALLIED movements
ALLIED retreat
AXIS Defence Lines

weather prevented air reconnaissance, which meant there was some uncertainty about the extent of German knowledge of the British movements. This was one of the problems, since lacking any sign of enemy activity or reaction, Cunningham was uncertain about the next step to take; his plan had been conceived in relation to an enemy reaction and subsequent troop movements, and lacking any sign of them there was little if anything that could be done. Technical unreliability also took its toll on the armoured forces, with the 7th Armoured Brigade down to 119 running tanks (more than 15 per cent breakdowns) and the 22nd Armoured Brigade down to 136 (12 per cent breakdowns). By the evening almost all the objectives for the day had been reached; XXX Corps had the 1st South African Division deployed on the track running south from Bir El Gubi, while the 7th Armoured Division's 22nd Brigade was some 50km to the south of it, the neighbouring 7th Armoured Brigade having reached and crossed the Trigh El Abd, the track from Bir El Gubi leading east to the frontier, and deployed north-west of Gabr Saleh. The 4th Armoured Brigade,

THE CAPTURE OF JALO

Oasis force carried out a diversion intended to distract the enemy attention from the true objectives of Operation Crusader. Moving across the desert from Jarabub, the force reached and seized the oasis of Jalo (some 150km south of Agedabia) with a pincer movement on 24–25 November 1941. The oasis was then used as a base by the Long Range Desert Group.

intended to screen the area between the 7th Armoured Division and the XIII Corps, stood on the Trigh El Abd, between Gabr Saleh and Sidi Omar, while XIII Corps' New Zealand and 4th Indian divisions had crossed the frontier line to the south of Sidi Omar, outflanking the Axis position along the frontier.

The morning of 19 November opened with uncertainty and critical decisions. Facing no visible German reaction, it was clear that the original plan of bringing the German armour to battle in the Gabr Saleh area needed amendments, and both General Gott, 7th Armoured Division commander, and General Norrie, XIII Corps commander, were loath to leave their armour sitting idle in the desert. Therefore both the 7th and the 22nd Armoured brigades were ordered to advance, 7th Support Group was to remain in the Gabr Saleh area to provide assistance if needed, and the 4th Armoured Brigade was to protect the flanks while screening the right wing of XXX Corps' advance. In the morning Gott appeared at the HQ of the 22nd Armoured Brigade and ordered an advance toward Bir El Gubi. This was a critical move, even with the benefit of hindsight. At that moment Gott had every reason to order the attack because the Ariete Division, the one deployed at Bir El Gubi, could not be left unmolested in the area, and also because it appeared a suitable target for the brigade to acquire some battlefield experience before clashing with the Germans. The 22nd Brigade attack against Bir El Gubi ran into the position defended by the Ariete Division, but this was not the easy victory that everybody had forecast. The Italian positions were overrun but, lacking infantry support (the brigade had only one 25-pounder battery), there were no troops to mop up the area, even when Italian soldiers holding one of the positions started to surrender. The Italians reacted and their medium tanks outflanked the Cruiser tanks of the 22nd Brigade, which was eventually compelled to withdraw. The Italians had lost thirty-four tanks while claiming the destruction of fifty of the enemy; the 22nd Brigade reported the loss of twenty-five, the difference (largely debated) being almost certainly made of the damaged ones. Much more importantly, the Italians had proven themselves a match for the Allies on the battlefield.

The 7th Armoured Brigade's advance was, however, completely uneventful. At about 1 p.m. the brigade approached Sidi Rezegh without having seen the enemy, and shortly thereafter seized the nearby airfield and captured nineteen Italian aircraft before deploying along the escarpment to the north. More or less, XIII Corps experienced a quite uneventful day too, its two divisions advancing north of the Sidi Omar. At the end of the day it seemed that events provided the necessary amendments to the Crusader plan; Cunningham decided to exploit the success in the north and ordered 7th Support Group to move to Sidi Rezegh, while the 1st South African Division was to move to Bir El Gubi, leaving one brigade ready to move to Sidi Rezegh. The 22nd Armoured Brigade was to move north of Bir El Gubi, while the 4th Armoured Brigade was to remain at Gabr Saleh.

'STRAFER' GOTT

General William Gott, commander of the British 7th Armoured Division since September 1941, acquired his nickname 'Strafer' while leading the Support Group during the Beda Fomm battle in February 1941. He became commander of the XIII Corps after Godwin-Austen relieved himself of command in February 1942.

On 18 November there were divided opinions in the German camp about the extent of the enemy movements; Rommel thought this was only a reconnaissance in force, while the Afrika Korps commander, General Ludwig Crüwell, was convinced that this was the beginning of a major offensive. Both German Panzer divisions lay idle in their positions, 15th Panzer east of Tobruk and close to the coast, and 21st Panzer on the Trigh Capuzzo, some 30km west of Sidi Azeiz. On the 19th Rommel did not change his opinion, but allowed 15th Panzer Division to be moved south-west of Gambut, along the Trigh Capuzzo, while a combat group of the 21st Panzer was to move toward Gabr Saleh. The combat group, with some eighty Panzers, clashed with the 4th Armoured Brigade in the evening, putting twenty-three M3 Stuart tanks out of action for the loss of two of their own, plus six damaged. At this point it was clear that the enemy was launching a major offensive, and on the 20th a decision was made to react and destroy the 4th Armoured Brigade moving toward the Trigh Capuzzo. Earlier the same day, both Panzer divisions were on the move and, trying to reach the flank of the enemy units, advanced to the south of the Trigh Capuzzo toward the frontier. However, the 21st Panzer

28. The US-built M3 light tank, also known as a 'Honey', which equipped the British 4th Armoured Brigade.

Division ran out of fuel and halted north of Sidi Omar, while the 15th Panzer Division (contrary to Rommel's orders) swung west and attacked the 4th Armoured Brigade, destroying another twenty-six Stuart tanks. By the evening the 22nd Armoured Brigade had moved east toward Gabr Saleh, while the 1st South African Division took up positions around Bir El Gubi, its 5th Brigade moving to support the 7th Armoured Brigade and the 7th Support Group against the German 90th Afrika Division at Sidi Rezegh. That same evening Cunningham approved the suggestion made by Gott and ordered the British 70th Division to start its breakout from Tobruk the morning after.

The First Battle of Sidi Rezegh (21–23 November)

21 November	Tobruk garrison attempts a breakout while the Afrika Korps moves toward Sidi Rezegh	
22 November	New Zealander Division attacks Sollum while Indian forces attack Sidi Omar. British 7th Armoured Division fights the first tank battle at Sidi Rezegh against the Afrika Korps	
23 November	End of the tank battle at Sidi Rezegh, with heavy casualties on both sides. The Afrika Korps attacks and destroys the 5th South African Brigade at the battle of the 'Sunday of the Dead'. The Italian CAM is put under Rommel's command	

The situation was still quite unclear for both sides on the morning of 21 November. While XIII Corps advanced west of the frontier, the 22nd and 4th Armoured brigades faced the 15th and 21st Panzer divisions in what looked like the beginning of the tank battle envisaged in the plan for Operation Crusader. At Sidi Rezegh, while the South African 5th Brigade approached, the 7th Support Group was deployed south of the escarpment with 7th Armoured Brigade to the rear, facing what was known as Point 175. On the night of 20/21 November the 70th Division started its breakout

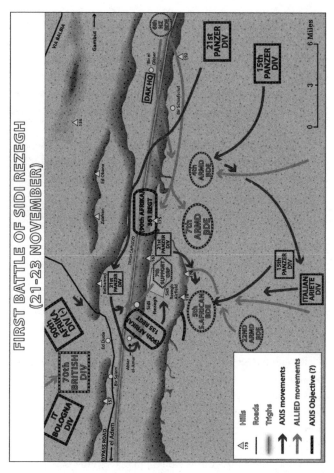

FIRST BATTLE OF SIDI REZEGH
(21–23 NOVEMBER)

from the Tobruk perimeter, while the 7th Support Group, with tank support from the 7th Brigade, attacked from Sidi Rezegh to seize the high ground dominating the Trigh Capuzzo. Soon, news came of an unexpected German move.

At 4 p.m. on the 20th, reports eventually enabled Rommel to get a clear picture of the situation, recognising that the main British effort was aimed at Sidi Rezegh. Since the strength of the enemy forces did not suggest a direct confrontation, a battle of

29. German Panzer III tanks moving across the desert. This was the German main battle tank throughout the Western Desert campaign.

movement was sought and the two Panzer divisions under the command of the Afrika Korps were redirected west to Sidi Rezegh. That same night the Afrika Korps started to move under cover of darkness, leaving behind a defence screen, and advancing toward Sidi Rezegh unseen by the two British armoured brigades. News of the arrival of the German Panzers reached 7th Armoured Division's units at Sidi Rezegh at 8 a.m., just before the attack toward the Trigh Capuzzo was to start; but since this could not be halted, given the imminent breakout from Tobruk, Brigadier Davy (in command of the area) took with him the 7th Hussars and the 2nd RTR to face the Panzers. This would result in a bitter day of battle at Sidi Rezegh. The 70th Division's breakout started at 8 a.m., and was faced with unexpected resistance not only from Italian troops, but also from the German 90th Afrika Division. Supported by the tanks of 32nd Armoured Brigade, the British units seized the enemy strongpoints one by one, before they were eventually halted by heavy artillery fire. By the afternoon a bridgehead some 4km deep and 4km wide had been established toward Ed Duda, and about 1,000 prisoners had been taken, half of them Germans.

At the same time as the breakout commenced, the attack by the 7th Armoured Division at Sidi Rezegh started with the infantry of the 7th Support Group crossing the escarpment toward Ed Duda, followed by the tanks of 6th RTR of the 7th Armoured Brigade; however, as soon as they started to cross the Trigh Capuzzo, German anti-tank and artillery fire inflicted horrendous casualties. Rommel, observing the situation first hand, ordered all the available artillery, anti-tank and 88mm Flak guns of the Afrika Korps under the command of General Böttcher to move forward; these started to destroy British tanks one by one, until 7th RTR withdrew back to the south of the escarpment after the loss of three-quarters of its tanks.

The deployment of the Afrika Korps to Sidi Rezegh was quite a gamble, as enemy units were able to redeploy at night virtually unnoticed. Captain Frey remembered the events: 'The division [15th Panzer] marched for 200 kilometres always with its flanks exposed. Once the enemy came from the south, then from the east, then again from the north. Who had no anti-tank weapons was done.'[10] Although the Panzer divisions lacked supplies themselves, the chasing 4th and 22nd brigades were to suffer greatly from supply troubles, as well as from the German rearguards and their anti-tank guns, and were delayed in their own movements. At about 8 a.m. the 15th and 21st Panzer divisions approached Sidi Rezegh, running into the British rear units that had started to evacuate the area in a hurry, unwittingly offering cover to the advancing Panzers. Facing the threat, Brigadier Davy deployed the 7th Hussars and the 2nd RTR to the east, unaware he was going to face almost the entire Afrika Korps. Heavy fighting lasted until the afternoon, when the 21st Panzer had practically destroyed all the 7th Hussars apart from ten tanks, while 2nd RTR's attempts to attack the flanks of the 15th Panzer Division were rebuffed by an anti-tank screen.

This is how Joe Lee, a driver with the 7th Armoured Brigade,

---

10 Frey, *Für Rommels Panzer durch die Wüste*, p. 107

30. An 88mm dual-purpose Flak gun firing. Its high silhouette made it a vulnerable target, but its range of almost 2km made it difficult to approach.

recollected the events: 'Later that afternoon we were halted among the wheeled transport, and the Brigadier and BM [Brigade Major] were in the ACV [armoured command truck], when without warning a vehicle burst into flames 100 yards or so away, and vehicles started to scatter in all directions. On came a German tank column with guns blazing. What a scramble! We had the ACV with the Brigadier and his staff on board to look after, and it was quite a job to keep between that and the enemy tanks. Taffy the Lap Gunner had to come up and fire the main armament, while Corporal Bill Rawlings (killed two days later) commanded. Utter chaos for a while, with vehicles going all ways, gunfire, smoke and dust. Remnants of the 2nd RTR were well into action, but I think it was just a matter of time before they and the 7th Hussars were virtually wiped out. The Brigadier and the BM piled into their tanks and off we went towards a cloud of dust and tanks moving in the distance. It was the 22nd Armoured Brigade, and we steamed flat out to them, the Brigadier waving a small white handkerchief. Stop! During the night we could see burning tanks, some glowing red, and the occasional spout of flame and sparks as ammunition caught fire, while the stench of burning oil and smoke wafted across the desert.'[11] While what was left of the British armour withdrew, General Crüwell pushed on to the Sidi Rezegh airfield, only to face determined British artillery fire, which prevented the Afrika Korps from advancing any further.

The first major tank battle between the Germans and the British was clearly won by the Panzers; at the end of the day 7th Armoured Brigade had twenty-eight tanks in running order, the 22nd Armoured Brigade had seventy-nine, and only the 4th Armoured Brigade remained at relatively full strength with 102 tanks (7th Armoured Division was left with 209 tanks out of 461). The 15th Panzer Division had 144 tanks (including forty-seven light and command ones), having suffered no losses, while the 21st Panzer Division was left with a total of fifty-seven tanks, thus almost bringing the Afrika Korps to parity with the 7th Armoured Division in terms of tanks. Worst of all, the situation remained unclear for Cunningham who, having lost radio contact with his leading units, lacked details and, on the basis of available reports, thought that the Afrika Korps was in fact withdrawing west and had lost some 170 of its tanks. As a consequence, orders were given to unleash the XIII Corps; Godwin-Austen was told to advance west at will, pushing the New Zealand Division forward with the result that, at the end of the day, its 6th Brigade was advancing along the Trigh Capuzzo west of Sidi Azeiz, and the

---

11   Forty, G., *Desert Rats at War 1*, p. 97

4th and 5th brigades were deployed to the north and south of the track.

The situation was indeed confusing; the British 70th Division was moving from the north toward Sidi Rezegh, facing Italian and German troops squeezed between it and the 7th Armoured Division in the south, who themselves were facing the Afrika Korps to the east and, to the west and south-west, units of the 90th Afrika Division. The 5th South African Brigade, approaching Sidi Rezegh from the south, had been halted short of its objective to avoid being caught in the melee. The view from the German side wasn't too encouraging either since the threat of the breakout from Tobruk was always present, as was the threat posed by the British 4th and 22nd Armoured brigades approaching from the east (plus the advance of the New Zealanders), while the situation at Sidi Rezegh was far from certain, with the possibility of an enemy attack from the south. Rommel ordered the 21st Panzer Division to seize Sidi Rezegh, while the 15th Panzer Division was to redeploy north toward Gambut, to get closer to its rear echelons.

On 22 November the 70th Division was ordered to continue with its breakout from Tobruk, while the 5th South African Brigade attacked 90th Afrika Division's positions around Point 178, south of Sidi Rezegh. The 70th Division only made limited progress, consolidating the bridgehead and eventually being halted in its advance because of the developments at Sidi Rezegh, while the 5th South African Brigade had a hard time at Point 178, eventually withdrawing after suffering 117 casualties and redeploying 3km south-east of the point. Rommel and Crüwell sensed an opportunity, and in the afternoon 21st Panzer Division attacked Sidi Rezegh, defended by the remnants of 7th Support Group and of the 7th and 22nd Armoured brigades, which had 107 tanks (4th Armoured Brigade had begun its pursuit of the 15th Panzer Division). Soon the battle turned into chaos, with 7th Support Group being overrun and both British armoured brigades suffering heavy losses. General Gott then decided to withdraw from Sidi Rezegh and redeploy around the 5th South African Brigade, with

31. South African troops close to a Marmon-Herrington armoured car, which was built in South Africa on a Ford chassis and often armed with a wide variety of weapons, including captured enemy ones.

the 22nd Armoured Brigade to the west and the 4th Armoured Brigade to the east. In the meantime, 15th Panzer Division, refuelling some 20km east of Sidi Rezegh, was ordered to attack an enemy column moving west. The division started moving first to the south, before swinging west and then north, running head on into the positions of the 8th Hussars of the 4th Armoured Brigade at dusk. This is how the war diary of the 15th Panzer Division described the events: 'The battalion commander recognised the vehicles as English tanks at ten yards. He burst through the enemy leaguer in his command vehicle and ordered No. 1 Company to go round to the left and No. 2 Company round the right to surround the enemy. The tanks put on their headlights and the commanders jumped out with their machine-pistols. Thus far there had been no firing. A few tanks tried to get away, but were at once set on fire by our tanks, and lit up the battlefield as bright as day. While the prisoners were being rounded up an English officer succeeded in setting fire to a tank.'[12] The German attack practically annihilated the regiment, destroying thirty-five tanks and taking more than 150 prisoners. The 4th Armoured Brigade dispersed and was not able to regroup before 24 November. The 7th Armoured Division, however, could still rely on forty-four tanks, but the Afrika Korps had 173 tanks in running order. News from the XIII Corps brought only limited respite to the British commanders, with the New Zealand Division taking Fort Capuzzo and blocking the Bardia–Tobruk road, while the 4th Indian Division seized Sidi Omar at the cost of thirty-seven infantry (mostly Matilda) tanks.

The day of 23 November was for the Germans the 'Sunday of the Dead', the Lutheran 'All Saints' Day'. There was hardly a more appropriate name given the events that were to occur. The day began with uncertain and diverging views on both sides of the front; Cunningham was now convinced the battle was becoming more and more an infantry matter and, on the 22nd, ordered the New Zealand Division to move toward Tobruk, while the XIII Corps was to contain the Bardia–Capuzzo area with the other units. Unaware of the true state of British armour, he ordered XXX Corps to support the New Zealand Division while maintaining its objective to defeat the enemy armour. Early the following day, still not fully aware of the events, Cunningham altered his orders and gave XIII Corps the task of taking over control of infantry

---

12 Lewin, R., *The Life and Death of the Afrika Korps*, p. 98

32. General Ludwig Crüwell, who took over command of the Afrika Korps from Rommel in August 1941, along with his chief of staff, Colonel Fritz Bayerlein.

operations against Tobruk, while XXX Corps' mission remained unaltered. Rommel's view of the situation was clearer, although strength and position of the enemy forces was still uncertain, and already in the afternoon of 22 November (even before the attack against the 4th Armoured Brigade) he decided to attack the enemy forces again with a massive blow. Early the following

33. A German Panzer IV tank moving past a destroyed Bren Gun Carrier. Armed with a short-barrelled 75mm gun, the Panzer IV was mainly intended for infantry support.

morning the bulk of the Afrika Korps was to strike south against the remnants of the 7th Armoured Division south of Sidi Rezegh toward Bir El Gubi, also to be attacked from Gambut by the Ariete Division. That same evening General Crüwell issued his orders, and at 7.30 a.m. the Afrika Korps began to advance.

The day began with a stroke of luck for the New Zealanders when the 6th Brigade ran into the bulk of the staff of the Afrika Korps left behind by Crüwell, who was now in the lead with a reduced staff as well as that of the 15th Panzer Division moving along the Trigh Capuzzo. After a brief fight, the New Zealanders easily destroyed the German staff detachment, taking some 200 prisoners, including many officers, and destroying a wealth of equipment such as radio and other communication instruments. The effects of this loss would become clearer in the days to follow.

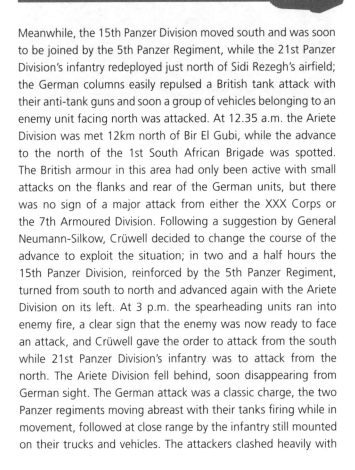

LUDWIG CRÜWELL

General Ludwig Crüwell, a cavalry officer who had served in the First World War on the Eastern and Western fronts, was given command of the 11th Panzer Division in August 1940. When he later took command of the Afrika Korps in September 1941 he was the most junior corps commander in the German Army.

Meanwhile, the 15th Panzer Division moved south and was soon to be joined by the 5th Panzer Regiment, while the 21st Panzer Division's infantry redeployed just north of Sidi Rezegh's airfield; the German columns easily repulsed a British tank attack with their anti-tank guns and soon a group of vehicles belonging to an enemy unit facing north was attacked. At 12.35 a.m. the Ariete Division was met 12km north of Bir El Gubi, while the advance to the north of the 1st South African Brigade was spotted. The British armour in this area had only been active with small attacks on the flanks and rear of the German units, but there was no sign of a major attack from either the XXX Corps or the 7th Armoured Division. Following a suggestion by General Neumann-Silkow, Crüwell decided to change the course of the advance to exploit the situation; in two and a half hours the 15th Panzer Division, reinforced by the 5th Panzer Regiment, turned from south to north and advanced again with the Ariete Division on its left. At 3 p.m. the spearheading units ran into enemy fire, a clear sign that the enemy was now ready to face an attack, and Crüwell gave the order to attack from the south while 21st Panzer Division's infantry was to attack from the north. The Ariete Division fell behind, soon disappearing from German sight. The German attack was a classic charge, the two Panzer regiments moving abreast with their tanks firing while in movement, followed at close range by the infantry still mounted on their trucks and vehicles. The attackers clashed heavily with

34. A German Panzer III command tank, used either by the 5th or 8th Panzer Regiment's headquarters.

the 5th South African Brigade, elements of the 7th Support Group, and the 4th and 7th Armoured brigades; the 22nd Armoured Brigade began an attack on the advancing German columns from the west.

Chaos and confusion reigned, guns fired, vehicles caught fire and added some light to the dusk, while the German columns lost orientation and started to disperse, following their instinct rather than their compass. The fight broke down into single units, sometimes single tanks or lorries. By 5 p.m. the two prongs of the German attack from the south and the north linked up at Sidi Rezegh's airfield, leaving a battlefield littered with wrecks, burning vehicles and corpses. Three-quarters of an hour later 15th Panzer Division's 115th Infantry Regiment swung east, meeting the spearheads of the 6th New Zealand Brigade approaching Sidi Rezegh. This is how Heinz Werner Schmidt, a company commander with the 115th Infantry Regiment, described the scene: 'We headed straight for the enemy tanks. I glanced back. Behind me was a fan of vehicles – a curious assortment of all types – spread out as far as the eye could see. There were armoured troops carriers, cars of various kinds, caterpillars hauling mobile guns, heavy trucks with infantry, motorised anti-aircraft units. Thus we roared onward to the enemy "barricade". I stared to the front fascinated. Right ahead was the erect figure of the colonel commanding the regiment. On the left close by and slightly in rear of him was the major's car. Tanks shells were whizzing through the air. The defenders were firing from every muzzle of their 25-pounders and their little 2-pounder anti-tank guns. We raced on at a suicidal pace. The battalion's commander car lurched on and stopped suddenly – a direct hit. I had just time to notice the colonel steadying himself. He turned sideways and dropped from the car like a felled tree. Then I had flashed past him. The major was still ahead.' 'Twilight came,' wrote Colonel Bayerlein, Afrika Korps' chief of staff, 'but the battle was still not over. Hundreds of burning vehicles, tanks and guns lit up the field of Totensonntag [the 'Sunday of the Dead']. It was long after midnight before we could get any sort of picture of the day's events, organise our force, count our losses and gains and form an appreciation of the general situation upon which the next day's operations would depend.'[13] The 'Sunday of the Dead' was over, but the battle was still raging.

Rommel's 'Dash to the Wire' (24–26 November)

24 November   Rommel, thinking the British armoured forces had been defeated, decides for a dash to the wire at the Libyan–Egyptian frontier. General Cunningham, commander of the Eighth Army, contemplates a withdrawal

---

13 Lewin, *The Life and Death of the Afrika Korps*, pp. 100–1

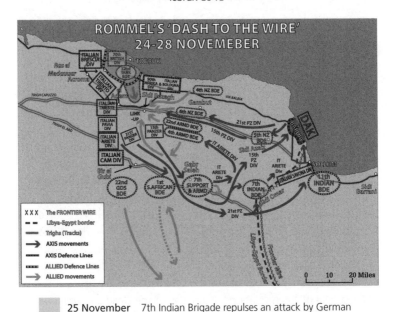

25 November		7th Indian Brigade repulses an attack by German Panzers at Sidi Omar, while the forces at Tobruk link up with the New Zealanders at Ed Duda. Auchinleck urges Cunningham to concentrate the attack in the Sidi Rezegh area
26 November		Axis forces moving back from the wire attack 5th New Zealand Brigade near Capuzzo. Auchinleck relieves Cunnigham from Eighth Army's command and replaces him with General Neil Ritchie

At dawn on the 24 November the battlefield offered images of defeat; the 5th South African Brigade had lost 3,394 men, which practically annihilated it as a combat unit, although around 2,300 men got back to the 1st South African Division. The 22nd Armoured Brigade had lost one-third of its thirty-four tanks, which, according to figures available to General Norrie, had the 7th Armoured Division down to some seventy-five tanks, even though the figure was likely to increase by repairs and by the 200 tanks held in reserve. German losses had been high too; apart from the infantry units,

35. Rommel pointing something out to his staff. During the winter battles of 1941–42 Rommel used to wear a leather overcoat and a civilian scarf, a gift from his sister.

which also lost many unit commanders, the two Panzer regiments had lost seventy-five Panzers, leaving the Afrika Korps with a total of ninety-two tanks, including thirty-four light and command ones. Nevertheless, the feeling that victory had been achieved rapidly spread amongst Axis troops; as Lieutenant Rebora wrote back home on 24 November: 'All our sacrifices, our privations, the blood of our fallen comrades will soon bear the crown of Victory! The day I shall write you from Cairo is not far away: the time of the English is over, like their rule here.'[14] A vision Rommel would share in full.

Rommel started his day early on 24 November; already before 4 a.m. he had a meeting with Colonel Westphal, his operation

14   Rebora, *Carri Ariete Combattono*, p. 135

officer, whom he told that the time had come to destroy what was left of the enemy before the remnants could withdraw back to Egypt. His idea was to take the lead of the Afrika Korps, including the Ariete Division, and perform a 'dash to the wire' (the barbed wire obstruction built by the Italians along the Libyan–Egyptian frontier) accompanied by General Gause, his chief of staff. His idea was that he would be back to the HQ that same evening, or the morning after at the latest. Westphal was to take over command of the rest of Panzergruppe Afrika and prevent any attempt to breakout from Tobruk. Basically, Rommel had decided to advance with his armoured units toward Sidi Omar in order to destroy its supply dumps and cut off the communication lines to its rear, which would have left the bulk of the enemy forces in Libya virtually surrounded and without supplies. Such an overly optimistic view was not shared by General Crüwell, who met Rommel at 6 a.m. at the HQ of the 21st Panzer Division; on the contrary, he thought that what was left of the enemy forces should be chased in the area between the Trigh Capuzzo and the Trigh El Abd and, while the area was mopped up, everything was to be recovered from the battlefield. Rommel did not change his mind, though, but rather insisted on his 'dash to the wire', adding that it was necessary to re-establish the situation at the Sollum front where, on the 23rd, the 5th Brigade had seized the Sollum barracks and effectively surrounded the Axis garrisons at Bardia and Sollum–Halfaya, while the 7th Indian Brigade had also made progress at Sidi Omar. In the meantime, the 4th Armoured Brigade, advancing west to meet the 6th Brigade which had already clashed with the Panzer near Sidi Rezegh, moved to occupy Gambut. Even Westphal and the intelligence officer of the Panzergruppe, Major von Mellenthin, did not share Rommel's optimistic view; in his post-war memoirs von Mellenthin wrote: 'Unfortunately Rommel overestimated his success and believed that the moment had come to launch a general pursuit … When he came back to El Adem [site of Panzergruppe Afrika HQ] he was in a state of excited exultation, and at once began to issue

36. German Panzers and armoured cars advancing. Apart from the single paved road, the via Balbia, and a few tracks, these columns had to rely on unmarked tracks which made orientation quite difficult.

orders which changed the whole character of the "Crusader" battle. In a signal which he dispatched to Berlin about midnight, Rommel said: "Intention for 24 November: a) To complete destruction 7th Armoured Division. b) To advance with elements of forces towards Sidi Omar with a view to attacking enemy on Sollum front."' When Rommel eventually left the HQ, Westphal and Mellenthin '… did not realize that this absence would last for several days and that we would only have the vaguest idea of where Rommel was or what he was doing.'[15]

The situation was not much better on the other side of the hill. General Norrie decided to regroup what was left of the XXX Corps around the 1st South African Division in order to refit and reorganise the 7th Armoured Division, and the 6th New Zealand Brigade was tasked with leading the advance towards Tobruk. Cunningham, however, was becoming increasingly anxious. In the morning of 23 November reports indicated that XXX Corps was left

15   von Mellenthin, F.W., *Panzer Battles*, p. 89.

with only forty-four tanks while the enemy still had approximately 120, and Auchinleck was forced to fly in from Cairo. The meeting took place in the afternoon, and Cunningham gave his pessimistic view of the situation: given the enemy superiority in armour, Eighth Army's infantry was exposed to tank attack and it was even possible that the Germans might be able to cut off the British formations in the Sidi Rezegh area, leaving nothing available to prevent any further advance into Egypt. Cunningham then asked Auchinleck whether it was time to halt the offensive and turn to the defensive. Auchinleck took the bold decision to continue with the offensive, which was sanctioned by a subsequent directive: 'You will therefore continue to attack the enemy relentlessly using all your resources even to the last tank. Your main objective will be as always to destroy the enemy tank forces. Your ultimate objective remains the conquest of Cyrenaica and then to advance on Tripoli …'[16] Immediately, Cunningham issued new orders; XIII Corps was to take over responsibility for the attack toward Tobruk, which also included the encircled garrison, and was given the immediate task of capturing Sidi Rezegh and Ed Duda. XXX Corps was to reorganise, deploying one South African brigade to relieve the Indian units along the frontier, while getting ready to protect the 1st South African Brigade and the advancing New Zealand Division from enemy tank attacks.

Rommel wanted the Afrika Korps to be ready to move at 10 a.m., which was indeed asking too much from men that had been fighting relentlessly until late the previous day. Nevertheless, the delay was minimal and at 10.30 a.m. the 21st Panzer Division set off, followed at 12.30 p.m. by the 15th Panzer Division. Both divisions were stretched out in long columns with open flanks, and were soon attacked by 7th Armoured Division's units, while the 1st South African Brigade halted the advance of the Ariete Division on the Trigh El Abd, east of Bir El Gubi. At 4 p.m. the spearheads of the 21st Panzer Division reached the frontier at Gasr El Abid, the

16 Playfair, I.S.O., *The Mediterranean and the Middle East III*, p. 52

division stretched over a distance of 70km, and the 15th Panzer Division approached the area south of Sidi Omar. Rommel, moving along with Gause in a staff car, was joined by Crüwell, himself moving in a staff car without protection, and both were to cross the frontier during the night of 24/25 November, spending it in Egypt surrounded by enemy troops. In the days that followed German operations along the frontier broke down into a series of small skirmishes, often determined more by Rommel's presence rather than by any specific directive or aim. Early on the 25th Rommel ordered the 15th Panzer Division to attack the enemy forces west of the Sollum–Halfaya front, while the 21st Panzer Division was to attack to the east, and the divisions were to converge at Sidi Omar. Advancing toward Sidi Azeiz, the 15th Panzer Division ran into a workshop unit of the British 1st Armoured Brigade repairing

37. A Crusader tank moving past a burning German Panzer IV tank. Operation Crusader led to the first large-scale tank battles in the Western Desert.

Matilda tanks; in spite of the limited serviceability of their tanks, the British crews fought tenaciously, but could not prevent the Germans from destroying sixteen Matilda tanks. During the rest of the day, the Germans mopped up the areas between Sidi Omar and Sidi Azeiz which was still in enemy hands. The 21st Panzer Division split into three groups, one moving toward Halfaya without meeting enemy forces and one moving further east, eventually running into a supply dump of XIII Corps where some prisoners and vital supplies were captured. The third group, made of the 5th Panzer Regiment, lost its orientation and ended up attacking the positions of the 7th Indian Brigade south of Sidi Omar, losing eight of its twenty-eight remaining Panzers. At 1 p.m. Rommel joined the regiment and ordered an attack on an enemy column moving south of Sidi Omar, but at the cost of seven more Panzers. In the meantime, the bulk of the 21st Panzer Division was halted by a lack of supplies south-east of the Halfaya Pass.

On 25–26 November Rommel and Crüwell began to develop a more coherent plan of attack; the main objectives were the enemy positions at Fort Capuzzo and Sidi Omar, restoring a supply line for the Bardia garrison, and the regrouping of the Afrika Korps now dispersed over a wide area. However, there also were two other critical factors: firstly, the lack of communications between Rommel and Panzergruppe Afrika HQ, mostly due to the loss of Afrika Korps' staff and its radios and communication equipment; and, secondly, the fact that two Panzer divisions were mostly relying on supplies from captured supply dumps (or even those from the beleaguered garrisons), since the German supply columns were unable to reach their units because the British forces had not withdrawn east as expected. The development of the situation is clearly described by Hellmuth Frey, the supply officer of the 15th Panzer Division: 'To supply our combat troops columns carrying fuel, ammunitions, food and water were put together. The convoy was expected to drive across the area from west to east behind the English held front protected by a few Panzer. Between 23 to 1 hours [11 p.m. to 1 a.m. on 25–26 November] the columns were loaded. Unfortunately they did never break through. Meanwhile the situation had changed again. While namely our Panzer marched toward south-east, an English formation took the same route back to the west without any of the two knowing a thing about the other. Now our columns must pull out. At dawn I moved along with some anti-tank guns toward the airfield [Sidi Rezegh], still in our hands in the evening. The English had moved west ... When I was back I found panic was spreading. Artillery fire on the road to Tobruk, on our back too. Our division in the east, new enemies in the west. Here too the enemy attack was blocked.'[17]

In a very short period of time, panic had spread on both sides of the front. In the morning of 24 November Cunningham told Norrie, who was at Gott's HQ near Gabr Saleh, that confidence had been restored since reports suggested that the Germans too had suffered heavy losses and only had a few tanks left. Just before noon Cunningham left Gott's HQ and flew back to Sidi Azeiz to meet Godwin-Austen. Two hours later a report about enemy tanks moving south-east was received from XXX Corps' HQ, but it only suggested that this was a nuisance rather than a full-scale attack. Back at Eighth Army's HQ, Cunningham met Auchinleck to examine the situation. Meanwhile, the arrival of the German Panzers spread panic amongst XXX Corps' support and logistics units on the frontier area, with many rushing back to the frontier and to Matruh, as noted in the British official history: 'Some lorries had never travelled so fast before.'[18] Auchinleck and Cunningham maintained calm within the ranks and took immediate measures; a force was to be organised from tanks held in reserve, while the 2nd South African Division was alerted for readiness and all the disorganised units retreating across the frontier were to be reorganised and returned.

However, on 25 November Auchinleck realised that although Cunningham had proved satisfactory until now, the Eighth Army's

---

17 Frey, *Für Rommels Panzer durch die Wüste*, p. 111

18 Playfair, *The Mediterranean and the Middle East III*, p. 54

GENERAL NEIL RITCHIE

Born in Guyana and commissioned in the Black Watch, he served in France and Mesopotamia during the First World War. After the war he served in India and in Palestine, and was a staff officer in the II Corps with the BEF in France in 1939–40, becoming the chief of staff of Middle East Command in May 1941.

commander was primarily thinking in terms of defence rather than attack. This loss of confidence led to Auchinleck's decision to remove Cunningham from command, a painful decision but also the right one in Auchinleck's view. On 26 November Auchinleck's chief of staff, General Neil Ritchie, took over command of the Eighth Army.

While Rommel was busy with his 'dash to the wire' and Eighth Army's HQ attempted to stabilise the front, developments on the battlefield were to take a new turn. On 23 November, when the battle of the 'Sunday of the Dead' was being fought south of Sidi Rezegh, the 24th and 25th battalions of the 6th New Zealand Brigade attacked the 90th Afrika Division at Point 175. The brigade eventually

38. Generals Charles Norrie and Neil Ritchie. Norrie took command of XXX Corps in October 1941 after its commander was killed in an air crash.

seized the position on 24 November, before advancing along the escarpment to the west and approaching Sidi Rezegh from the north. Meanwhile, the 5th New Zealand Brigade, along with the bulk of the 1st Army Tank Brigade (with eighty-six infantry tanks), approached the area from the Trigh Capuzzo. On the 25th, while the Afrika Korps was raiding the frontier area, both New Zealand brigades advanced westward from the north and south of the Trigh Capuzzo, reaching the Sidi Rezegh airfield and approaching Belhamed. These were the troops that took Hellmuth Frey's supply columns by surprise. At this point Godwin-Austen, in charge of operations in the Tobruk area, ordered the New Zealand Division to capture Sidi Rezegh, Belhamed and Ed Duda, while the 70th Division was to renew its breakout attempt and link up with the New Zealanders. Facing Kampfgruppe Böttcher, commanded by General Karl Böttcher and formed of a mixture of units from the 90th Afrika and Italian Brescia divisions plus Afrika Korps' artillery, the New Zealanders attacked at 9 p.m. and fought hard against elements of the 155th and 361st Afrika regiments. The 4th New Zealand Brigade eventually seized Belhamed between 1 and 2 a.m. on 26 November. However, the advance of the 6th New Zealand Brigade was halted by a mixed group of Italian Bersaglieri (marksmen) and infantry while crossing the escarpment leading north to the Trigh Capuzzo, which blocked the entire division from advancing to Ed Duda at first light.

The hard fighting that day, which broke down into a series of skirmishes, is described in Lieutenant H. Smith's recollections of the 21st New Zealand Battalion, spearheading the advance to Sidi Rezegh mosque: approaching he 'saw a man on the skyline shaking his blanket and others moving around', then 'I sent two men towards them to see who they were. They were Jerries and dug in. They didn't waste time but opened fire straight away with machine guns and rifles as soon as they saw us. I told the men to fix bayonets and was pleased to see them drop to the ground as one to do this. They waited till I told them and then away we went up the hill. It was a bloody do with grenades and bayonets.

When the area was cleared we went on but more slowly as we had wounded and some prisoners.'[19]

At this point General Scobie, 70th Division commander, decided to start the breakout on his own initiative and attacked south at noon with the 32nd Tank Brigade in the lead, accompanied by the 1st Essex Regiment and a company of the Royal Northumberland Fusiliers. The breakout succeeded, and by 3 p.m. on the 26th Ed Duda was in British hands. This is how Lieutenant Philip Brownless of C Company, the Essex Regiment, recalled the events: 'As we advanced over the top [of Ed Duda escarpment], shells were bursting everywhere. The road was 150 yards in front, with a continuous storm of shells bursting down its length, and knocking the telegraph poles about like pea-sticks. I kept shouting to the sections to keep well spaced. We reached the road, which was our objective. There were some deafening explosions as shells landed right amongst the platoon. I was blown over, and so were some others. I felt myself and was surprised to find that I was all right. I could not see a thing … I shouted "Advance!" and moved a hundred yards forward of the road, made the platoon get down, and placed my sections, one covering the road and the other two forward.'[20] Later on, at 10.45 p.m., a squadron of the 44th RTR advancing from the east made contact with the breakout forces

KNIGHT'S CROSSES AT TOBRUK

Amongst those who won the Knight's Cross medal for their role in the winter battle was Colonel Fritz Bayerlein, chief of staff of the Afrika Korps, General Karl Böttcher, commander of the Artillery Command 104, and Colonel Hans-Levin von Barby, commander of the 361st 'Afrika' Regiment of 90th 'Afrika' Division.

19 Murphy, W.E., *Relief of Tobruk. Official History of New Zealand in the Second World War 1939–45*, p. 276

20 Lyman, *Siege*, p. 275

39 . Afrika Korps' soldiers in a typical battle scene. The swastika flag on the truck's bonnet was used for air identification, since 'friendly fire' was quite common in the Western Desert.

from Tobruk, followed at 1 a.m. on the 27th by the 19th New Zealand Battalion. That same morning the 6th New Zealand Brigade seized Sidi Rezegh and opened the way toward the Trigh Capuzzo. The siege of Tobruk had been broken.

Facing crisis on the Tobruk front, Westphal sent a message to Crüwell at 3 p.m. on 26 November clearly stating that enemy forces with tank support were attacking the rear and the right wing of Kampfgruppe Böttcher's positions, while air reconnaissance had spotted enemy armour approaching from Gabr Saleh. The message concluded with a simple question: 'Where are our Panzer?'[21] At the frontier Crüwell had been organising the attack at Sidi Omar, while the 15th Panzer Division prepared to attack Sidi Azeiz. Neither attacks were carried out, and instead the bulk of the 21st Panzer Division was ordered to attack and break through the positions held by the 28th New Zealand (Maori) Battalion at Sollum, reaching the Axis garrison at Bardia. In the afternoon

21 von Taysen, A., *Tobruk 1941*, p. 268

the 15th Panzer Division's 115th Infantry Regiment attacked Fort Capuzzo, but developments at Tobruk forced Rommel to change his plans; having realised that it was not possible to destroy the enemy forces at Sollum–Halfaya he called the attack off at 9 p.m. on the 26th (Capuzzo was attacked again the following day by 33rd Engineer Battalion, which withdrew after heavy losses). Rommel then ordered the 21st Panzer Division to move at once toward El Adem and, from there, to Tobruk; the 15th Panzer Division was to follow, after attacking a known enemy supply dump near Sidi Azeiz. The following morning both divisions were on the move and the 15th Panzer Division eventually attacked and destroyed the HQ of the 5th New Zealand Brigade, taking some 700 prisoners, and killing or wounding more than ninety. This was Rommel's one and only success during his three-day 'dash'.

The Second Battle of Sidi Rezegh (27 November–2 December)

27 November	Rommel orders the Afrika Korps westward to attack British XXX Corps at Sidi Rezegh. 15th Panzer Division seizes Sidi Azeiz	
28 November – 2 December	The Afrika Korps attacks the New Zealanders at Sidi Rezegh, who are eventually forced to withdraw and are replaced by the 4th Indian Division	

One of the consequences of Rommel's 'dash' was the time it allowed 7th Armoured Division to recover, which now had seventy-seven M3 Stuart tanks in its 4th Armoured Brigade and forty-two Cruisers in the 22nd Armoured Brigade, both deployed east of Bir El Gubi and Sidi Rezegh (the 7th Armoured Brigade was sent back to Egypt to refit). The division lacked artillery and so the depleted 7th Support Group was broken down into Jock columns. The Afrika Korps was now made of a largely depleted 21st Panzer Division and a 15th Panzer Division with only fifty Panzers, seventeen of which were light or command ones. At 1.10 p.m. on 27 November the 15th Panzer Division was attacked south-west of Gambut by

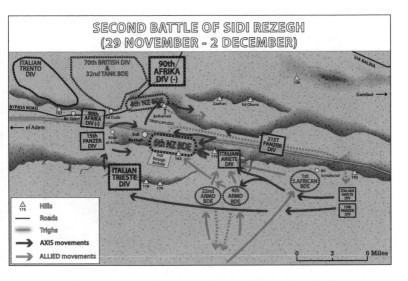

the 22nd Armoured Brigade, joined by the 4th Armoured Brigade at about 4 p.m.; both posed a serious threat to the German columns until 6.30 p.m. when, much to the Germans' surprise, they withdrew at dusk. The British armour leaguered south, and the lack of infantry and artillery prevented them from blocking the road while the Germans slipped west to leaguer themselves south of Point 175; they had lost thirteen Panzers to fourteen British tanks, but the road to Tobruk was now open. Meanwhile, the Ariete Division was making its way back to join the 15th Panzer Division, still equipped with around seventy medium tanks. At the end of the day, Rommel decided to regroup his forces and reconnoitre the area to the west before formulating a plan of escape.

On 28 November both sides consolidated their positions and regrouped, while the New Zealanders and the Tobruk garrison widened the corridor along the escarpment north of the Trigh Capuzzo to the west. By nightfall a firm line had been established, with its main strongpoint at Zanfran and Belhamed along the northern escarpment while, on the escarpment south of the Trigh Capuzzo, Point 175 and the Sidi Rezegh airfield formed a line

40. Bren Gun Carriers of the 7th Armoured Division, the 'Desert Rats'. In 1940 this was the best armoured unit in the Western Desert.

to the west, although this was interrupted along the southern escarpment by the positions held by Kampfgruppe Böttcher at Point 178 and Bir Bu Cremisa. Ed Duda, close to the bypass road built around Tobruk, still remained as the main stronghold of the Tobruk breakout. Once again, Rommel and Crüwell had diverging opinions about the next move to take; the latter took into account the actual disposition on the ground and ordered an east to west attack along the escarpments, with the 21st Panzer Division moving toward Belhamed, the 15th Panzer Division seizing Ed Duda from the gap in the escarpments to the south, the 90th Afrika Division attacking the corridor from the north, and the Ariete Division taking Point 175. Rommel preferred a north to west attack with all the available units moving from the north of Belhamed, and sent Crüwell a message at 9 a.m. on the 28th, but the latter, who had already issued his orders at 8 a.m., decided that the order could not be altered. During the afternoon the 15th Panzer Division approached Sidi Rezegh, overrunning a New Zealand dressing station and rescuing

41. Generals Bernard Freyberg VC (left) and Claude Auchinleck (right). Freyberg was to lead the New Zealand Division throughout the North African and Italian campaigns.

800 German prisoners from a camp. A move also favoured by 1st South African Brigade's failure to reach and secure, as ordered, Point 175. The brigade halted less than 20km from its objective, while during the night XIII Corps' and New Zealand Division's HQs moved into Tobruk, with the exception of General Freyberg (New Zealand Division's commander) and a small staff. That was a sound move given the high casualty rate of commanding officers, and the following day General von Ravenstein, 21st Panzer Division's commander, went missing with his car and was captured (replaced by General Böttcher, who was later replaced by Colonel Mickl).

The German attack on 29 November, which started the second battle of Sidi Rezegh, did not begin well; the 15th Panzer Division moved early, switching south along the southern escarpment toward Point 178 and the positions of Kampfgruppe Böttcher, renamed Kampfgruppe Mickl, and reached it at around noon. In the north, the 21st Panzer Division moved slowly and only at dusk reached its starting positions at Zanfran. The Ariete Division, despite being continuously attacked by the British armour protecting the 1st South African Brigade, was much more successful; in the late afternoon the Italian division approached the positions at Point 175, where New Zealand troops were waiting for the arrival of the South Africans. Uncertainty about the actual nationality of the approaching troops allowed the Italians to penetrate the defence perimeter and to open fire against the defenders; at 5.10 p.m. the commander of 21st New Zealand Battalion sent an urgent message to the brigade HQ: 'They are into my lines with three tanks and are taking prisoners. Arty support at once for Gods sake.'[22] Soon overwhelmed, the New Zealanders were compelled to abandon their position and withdraw, eventually to realise that the Italians, who believed Point 175 was in German hands, were as shocked as they were by the events.

At about 2 p.m. the 15th Panzer Division attacked Ed Duda from the south-west, managing to advance along the bypass road and seize the western end of the position, now defended by a mixture

42. A German Fieseler Storch (stork) reconnaissance plane has landed close to a motorised column of the Afrika Korps.

22   Murphy, *The Relief of Tobruk*, p. 401

SIDI REZEGH'S VCs

No less than four Victoria Crosses were awarded for exceptional valour at Sidi Rezegh: 2nd Lieutenant G. Ward Gunn of Royal Horse Artillery, Rifleman J. Beeley of the King's Royal Rifle Corps, Captain P.J. Gardner of the Royal Tank Regiment and Brigadier J.C. 'Jock' Campbell commanding the 7th Support Group.

of British and Australian troops. However, thanks to artillery support the German attack was halted, and the positions regained during the night with the help of British tanks. On 29 November the 15th Panzer Division still had forty-three tanks (of which fifteen were light and command ones), but these were down to thirty-six the following day (including eleven light tanks), while the depleted 21st Panzer Division was left with twenty-three tanks, including eight light and command ones. There would not be a second chance for the Afrika Korps this time. Air reconnaissance again brought bad news for the Germans on the morning of 30 November, as enemy forces had been spotted to the south, gathering and preparing to move north to counterattack. At this point Rommel ordered his forces to close the Tobruk corridor, set up a defensive perimeter to the south, while Kampfgruppe Mickl and the Ariete Division were given the task of seizing Sidi Rezegh. The 15th Panzer Division was to support Kampfgruppe Mickl attacking to the west, while the 21st Panzer and the 90th Afrika divisions were to attack from the east and the north.

The day was a succession of attacks and counterattacks, and at about 3 p.m. the 15th Panzer Division and Kampfgruppe Mickl attacked the 24th and 26th New Zealand battalions at Sidi Rezegh, just south of the Trigh Capuzzo; they resisted for hours, but were overrun at dusk and suffered some 600 casualties. The 21st Panzer Division's attack south of Zanfran started at around 5 p.m. and ended without success, even though the defence to the south, held by the Ariete Division, managed to prevent the 1st South African Division from reaching Sidi Rezegh's airport and held the British armour at bay, which was unable to mount a counterattack. Early in the morning of 1 December, 15th Panzer Division continued its attack west from Sidi Rezegh to Belhamed, defended by the 4th New Zealand Brigade. After two hours of fighting the New Zealanders' positions were overrun again, leaving Belhamed to the Germans and effectively cutting the New Zealand Division in two. Later in the morning, fearing a German attack against the positions of the 6th New Zealand Brigade which was deployed between Belhamed and the Trigh Capuzzo, the British 4th Armoured Brigade moved north to join it; they had just reached the position when the New Zealanders were ordered to withdraw. The 4th Armoured Brigade thought the New Zealanders were to move southward but, with the Sidi Rezegh airfield under Axis artillery fire, they actually moved east toward Zanfran and the bulk of the division (4th Armoured Brigade withdrew south). By 1 p.m. the withdrawal was complete, but after

43. Armour of the Italian Ariete Division moving in open desert.

one hour Freyberg realised that his troops, squeezed between the 15th and 21st Panzer divisions, plus the Ariete Division, had no other alternative than to withdraw from the area to rest and refit. General Norrie agreed to the decision, subsequently approved by General Ritchie, and under cover of darkness the New Zealanders withdrew west, eventually reaching the Libyan–Egyptian frontier on 2 December.

Following their failure to dislodge the Ariete and the 21st Panzer divisions from their positions around Point 175, the 1st South African Brigade withdrew south along with the British 4th Armoured Brigade that same night. The Tobruk corridor had been cut, but the British 70th Division was determined to hold the Ed Duda strongpoint. By now, however, the supply situation for Rommel and the Axis forces had worsened beyond repair; the British interdiction of the sea lanes across the Mediterranean had cut supplies to the Axis forces steadily since September, and the climax of the crisis was reached in December. That month only 1,700 troops arrived in Libya, compared to 4,800 in November and 12,700 in September, along with 47,600 tons of supplies compared to 79,200 in November, 92,400 in October and 94,000 in September. The fuel situation was even worse, with only 7,600 tons reaching Libya in December compared to 31,700 in November, 15,100 in October and 17,700 in September. In the meeting Rommel had with the Italian commander in Libya, General Ettore Bastico, the former remarked that the battle had now turned into one of attrition and, while the Axis could not make good their losses, the enemy could and already were. In fact, Ritchie had already activated the 2nd South African Division, now moving to the frontier to relieve the 4th Indian Division, and with new and refitted forces at his disposal, Ritchie was now thinking of attacking El Adem, to the south of Tobruk, which would have seriously threatened the Axis forces with encirclement and defeat. Even though Rommel knew from his intelligence that an enemy attack would not start before 3 December, there were only limited options at his disposal.

Concerned by the situation in Bardia and along the frontier, Rommel decided to probe again in that direction but, given the lack of Panzers, it was limited to two battalion-sized combat groups that advanced along the Trigh Capuzzo and the via Balbia on 3 December; they were soon ambushed by the 5th New Zealand Brigade. Meanwhile, Ritchie's plan was taking shape and on the 3 December Norrie ordered the 11th Indian Brigade, supported by the 8th RTR (with sixteen infantry tanks), to seize the village of Bir El Gubi, from which they were to advance further towards El Adem. In the morning of 4 December the 21st Panzer Division attacked Ed Duda but, even before any progress was made, Rommel called the attack off due to an enemy advance toward Bir El Gubi, which was only defended by

44. A German half-tracked SdKfz 250/3 command vehicle, mostly used for communications and observation purposes.

a mixed Italian reconnaissance unit. Bir El Gubi was attacked on the night of 4/5 December and its defenders, the Italian 'Young Fascist' Battalion, held out while Rommel switched the 15th and 21st Panzer divisions, followed by the Italian Ariete and Trieste divisions, from the east of Tobruk to the south-west to meet the new threat. The Afrika Korps was able to push the 11th Indian Brigade (still fighting at Bir El Gubi) back, but the delayed arrival of the two Italian divisions, only reaching Bir El Gubi on 7 December, and the further strengthening of the XXX Corps made any further attempts to counterattack pointless. At this point Rommel made the decision he had been considering during the last two days, which was to withdraw the Axis forces west of Tobruk to the Gazala line. The Italians opposed him, but the situation on the battlefield and the lack of reinforcements and supplies left no other choice; on 8 December the Axis forces started to disengage and to withdraw to the west. The 'Crusader' battle was over.

AFTER THE BATTLE:
THE WINNERS AND THE LOSERS

Rommel Back to El Agheila

1–3 December	Sporadic fighting in the Sidi Rezegh area, while Ritchie brings forward reinforcements and new troops arrive
4–5 December	Rommel's last drive against the Tobruk garrison ends in failure. On 5 December he is alerted to the worsening supply situation for the Axis forces
7 December	In spite of Italian opposition, Rommel orders withdrawal to the Gazala line some 15km west of Tobruk
10 December	The Tobruk siege is lifted, the Axis forces withdraw west
15 December	British attack against the Gazala line, Rommel orders a full retreat back to El Agheila, which starts the following day
24 December	British forces enter Benghazi
28–30 December	Afrika Korps holds off the British armour at Mersa Brega, effectively halting the Eighth Army's advance

The end of the 'Crusader' battle did not mean the end of the winter battle, which lasted for some time. Between 11 and 16 December the Axis forces had redeployed to the Gazala line running to the west of Tobruk: the Italian infantry in the north, then the Italian mobile forces and, further to the south, the Afrika Korps. On 10 December, after eight months, the siege of Tobruk came to an end following the withdrawal of the Italian divisions to the west of the perimeter. Delaying tactics successfully halted XXX Corps' pursuit, which didn't reach the Gazala line until 13 December. Following a reorganisation of Eighth Army's chain of command on 9 December, XXX Corps was given the task of dealing with Axis forces on the Libyan–Egyptian frontier, while XIII Corps would control operations aimed at driving the enemy out of Cyrenaica. The British attack started on 15 December with the 5th New Zealand and the Polish brigades trying to break through the Italian positions just to the south of Gazala, and the 4th Indian Division attacking the Trieste and Ariete positions at Alam Hamza, the key strongpoint. Both attacks were unsuccessful, and hopes were pinned on an outflanking manoeuvre by 4th Armoured Brigade, which was to strike deeply behind the Axis lines at Bir Haleig and Tmimi. However, the limited range of the M3 Stuart tanks delayed the brigade, which only reached Bir Haleig on the afternoon of 15 November. Only on the following day was the brigade able to push forward to Tmimi and face the Afrika Korps, although little damage was inflicted and no serious threat was posed to an enemy that, as it was now clear, was preparing to withdraw further west. That same night the Axis forces pulled out of the line and headed west, into the Jebel Akhdar, unhindered by British armour.

Rommel's decision to withdraw caused a great stir in the Italian high command, which was in charge of the whole area; while the Italians wanted to defend the positions west of Tobruk in order to keep Benghazi under control, Rommel wanted to withdraw back to the starting positions of his first drive into Cyrenaica during the previous April. A compromise was reached, with the bulk of the Axis forces left to defend the Gazala line, while the 90th Afrika Division was sent back to Agedabia to protect the lines of communication. Furthermore, the troops deployed at Bardia and Sollum–Halfaya, who Rommel had asked to be evacuated by sea, had to remain in place, although no one quite knew how they were to be supplied. Two more commanders fell victim both to Rommel's fury and the war itself; on 10 December the Italian General Gastone Gambara, commander of the Corpo d'Armata di Manovra, was replaced by General Piazzoni after a heated clash with Rommel, while during the same night the 90th Afrika Division's commander, General Max Sümmermann, was killed in an air attack. The battle was still not over. On the night of 16/17 December the Axis forces on the Gazala line withdrew following Rommel's orders, which clearly stated that the whole of Cyrenaica was to be evacuated back to the Agedabia–El Agheila positions. This was a clear consequence of the danger posed by being exposed in such an area, as the Italians had learned bitterly in February 1941, and eventually the Italian commanders agreed to impose a slow withdrawal in order to rescue and save as much materiel as possible from the area.

Trying to avoid being caught in a trap, Rommel had the Italian forces, mostly on foot, moving along the via Balbia coastal road towards Agedabia, while the Afrika Korps was to move inland, first to El Mechili and then back to Benghazi. The first stage of the withdrawal went smoothly, with the Italians reaching the Derna area by 17–18 December, and the Afrika Korps also reached El Mechili. Facing the enemy withdrawal, General Ritchie decided on a full-scale pursuit; he sent the 4th Indian Division north along the coast to try to block the road of the Italian withdrawal, while the 7th Armoured Division was sent west to El Mechili. Acting independently, the 22nd Guards Brigade Group (renamed 'Bencol'), was to drive into the desert towards Benghazi, with the aim of seizing and holding the port city. The advance of the Eighth Army's columns was greatly hampered by the climate, with its winter rains, and by a series of demolitions carried out by the retreating Axis forces; only on the 18th did the 7th Armoured Division approach El Mechili, while the 4th Indian Division approached Derna and Lamluda to the west, but were unable to halt the enemy withdrawal. The Bencol force was only able to

45. *General Erwin Rommel, who since August 1941 commanded the Panzer Group Afrika, along with his chief of staff, General Alfred Gause (left). The difference in uniforms is remarkable.*

move on 20 December, and by then the Axis forces had already withdrawn further back to the west, making it very obvious that they did not want to make a stand at Derna or El Mechili; for this reason Ritchie altered Bencol's mission, which was now to push west and prevent an enemy escape from the Cyrenaica bulge. By 23 December Eighth Army's columns had made fast progress, reaching Barce, Benina (east of Benghazi), Soluch and Antelat (both south of Benghazi), and threatened to cut off Rommel's retreat. Most of the Axis units were already slipping away from the trap, however, and uncertainty about the positions of enemy units (in order to gain speed these columns were down to the barest essentials, often lacking strength and supplies, and hampered by overstretched lines of communication) made a repetition of Beda

46. The commander-in-chief Middle East, General Sir Claude Auchinleck, with his chief of staff, General Neil Ritchie, who replaced Cunningham as Eighth Army's commander on 26 November 1941.

Fomm practically impossible. On 23 December the 15th Panzer Division spotted and attacked an approaching column of the Coldstream Guards and, despite support from the 3rd RTR, the British column was pushed back to the east of Antelat, withdrawing after the arrival of the bulk of the 7th Armoured Division's Support Group. By then the Italian units had already slipped away from the trap and started to build a defence line at Agedabia, soon to be joined by the Afrika Korps.

Having not accurately assessed the situation, Ritchie and Godwin-Austen sent their units to clear the area south of Benghazi, while the Axis forces consolidated their positions around Agedabia. Only the following day did the situation become clearer, and Godwin-Austen ordered the 22nd Guards Brigade to attack the enemy positions on 26–27 December; however, the enemy resisted fiercely and the attack ended with a failure.

Similarly, the first major tank battle since the Axis withdrawal followed on the 28th, ending in another British withdrawal. Having regained confidence, both Rommel and Crüwell decided to defeat the enemy armour piecemeal and, having noticed a gap in the enemy deployment, sent the 15th and 21st Panzer divisions (with a total of about sixty tanks, including forty-two medium) against the 22nd Armoured Brigade to the south of Agedabia at El Haseiat. The Germans won the day, destroying thirty-seven out of ninety British tanks (thirty-five M3 Stuarts, the rest Cruiser tanks), at the cost of seven of their own. The attack was renewed on 30 December, and again it ended in victory for the German forces: twenty-three out of sixty-two British tanks were destroyed or damaged, at the cost of seven Panzers. The 22nd Armoured Brigade was withdrawn to rest and refit. Axis forces did the same, after Rommel decided to hold out at Agedabia longer than he had forecast. At this point there was little that Ritchie could do apart from try to regroup his forces and prepare for a full-scale assault against the enemy positions. However, it was clear that, this time, Rommel was not going to wait for it.

On 1 January 1942 the first Axis units began to withdraw from the Agedabia positions, moving further west back to El Agheila where, since 5 January, Italian troops had started to establish a defence line to the south of Mersa Brega. Axis movements went unnoticed at first, and only on 5 January did the British forces realise that a major withdrawal was taking place. The following

THE LESSONS OF OPERATION CRUSADER

After the experience he had with the 7th Armoured Division during Operation Crusader, General Auchinleck decided to reorganise Eighth Army's armour around the concept of the 'brigade group'. This concept allowed for a more balanced organisation, with the tank regiment now supported by a motor infantry battalion, an artillery regiment and all necessary support units.

day the bulk of the Afrika Korps and of the other Axis forces at Agedabia pulled back west, protected by a sandstorm, reaching the El Agheila defence line in three days and redeploying in the area by mid-January. The positions at El Agheila were not only heavily defended, but were also practically impassable, protected by salt marshes and by soft sand areas, unsuitable for both wheeled and even tracked vehicles. It was to become clear that no advance further west was possible for the Eighth Army, which was now itself suffering from fatigue and a lack of adequate supplies. The winter battle was over; Auchinleck had succeeded in reconquering Cyrenaica, but was still a long way from threatening Tripoli and from putting an end to the war in the Western Desert.

Summing Up: The End at Bardia and Sollum

1 January	Rommel orders retreat to the positions at El Agheila	
2 January	Axis garrison at Bardia surrenders	
17 January	Axis garrisons at Sollum and Halfaya surrender	

Rommel's decision to withdraw west of Tobruk also had another consequence, which was leaving the beleaguered garrisons of Bardia and Sollum behind, surrounded by enemy forces and hard to reach for supply and evacuation by sea. Since 9 December General Norrie's XXX Corps had been given the task of dealing with these two pockets, and Norrie handed this task over to General de Villiers and his 2nd South African Division, still largely untrained. At Bardia there were some 2,200 Germans, mostly from the rear area command, plus about 6,600 Italians, while the garrisons of Sollum and Halfaya, along with the two smaller strongpoints west of the Halfaya named 'Faltenbacher' and 'Cirener', included some 4,200 Italian soldiers of the Savona Division and 2,100 Germans, mostly from 1st Battalion of the 104th Infantry Regiment led by Major Wilhelm Bach. The first attack on 16 December, led by the 3rd South African Brigade against the northern and southern

WILHELM BACH

A Lutheran pastor, Wilhelm 'Papa' Bach was a First World War volunteer who fought on the Western Front until captured by the British on 21 October 1916. Recalled to duty he fought against France in 1940 and was subsequently transferred to the 104th Regiment where he became a battalion commander shortly after it arrived in Libya.

47. *War without hate: an Australian 'digger' is helping a wounded Italian prisoner of war to the truck that will take him and his comrades to the POW camp.*

end of the Bardia perimeter proved that the enemy was willing and determined to resist despite the odds. After two days of fighting and lacking any result, de Villiers called the attack off and prepared for another, which was to be supported by the New Zealand Division's Cavalry Regiment (equipped with light tanks and Bren carriers), and by the 8th and 44th RTR equipped with Valentine and Matilda tanks, plus naval gunfire support.

The new attack began on New Year's Eve 1941, this time with the 3rd and 4th South African brigades attacking from the south-west and facing heavy resistance, including a local Axis counterattack that overran a battalion HQ. A new effort was made after darkness fell on 1 January 1942, this time with the tanks of 44th RTR leading the advance. In spite of fierce opposition on the enemy side, the garrison of Bardia surrendered on 2 January and a total of 7,982 enemy soldiers (including 1,804 Germans) were taken prisoner at the cost of 139 killed and 295 wounded. In addition, 1,171 prisoners of war, mostly New Zealanders (650), were released from captivity and a large amount of supplies was also captured. Axis positions at Halfaya and Sollum were then heavily bombed in an attempt to achieve a bloodless surrender, but these too had to be taken by force; on 11 January the 6th South African Brigade attacked lower Sollum, seizing it the following day and cutting the other enemy groups off from the sea and their only water supply. Lacking supplies, the other garrisons had no other option than to surrender (with Rommel's permission), which they did on 17 January. The surrender of Sollum added another 2,126 German and 3,413 Italian prisoners, for a total of 13,842 enemy troops taken prisoner in the frontier area between December 1941 and January 1942, at the cost of 600 casualties.

Rommel's final withdrawal to El Agheila and the surrender of the Bardia and Sollum–Halfaya garrisons put an end to the 'winter battle'; it was a costly defeat for the Axis side, with a total of 14,760 German and about 23,700 Italian combat casualties (including the beleaguered garrisons), and an even greater loss of manpower if non-combat casualties are also included. These brought the totals to about 42,000 Italians and 20,698 German troops lost between November 1941 and January 1942, meaning a loss of around 60 per cent of the Axis troops in Cyrenaica. Of these, 2,300 were killed (1,100 Germans), 6,100 wounded (3,400 Germans) and 29,900 went missing (10,100 Germans). Weapons,

48. Italian prisoners of war are being escorted to a POW camp. During Operation Compass some 130,000 Italian troops were taken prisoner, making it a victory comparable to that obtained by the Germans in France in 1940.

equipment and transport losses were equally high, with the Germans having lost a total of 229 Panzers (sixty of which were light or command ones, plus 135 Panzer III and thirty-four Panzer IV medium tanks), plus sixty-three medium and 187 light tanks lost by the Italians. Eighth Army losses were much less, with 2,900 killed, 7,300 wounded and 7,500 missing for a total of 17,700 troops, or 15 per cent of the total strength (worth noting is that more than a quarter of these, 4,620, were from the New Zealand Division). Tank losses are hard to assess, but on 1 January 1942 Eighth Army had lost about 600 tanks either because of enemy action or breakdowns (other sources give about 800), although by 12 December 456 of these had been recovered from the battleground and 231 of them had been repaired, plus some other fifty under repair, which suggests a total loss of about 320 tanks.

Rommel's Second Drive into Cyrenaica

21 January	Rommel starts his second drive into Cyrenaica
29 January	Axis forces seize Benghazi, while a feint is aimed at El Mechili
4–6 February	Rommel's forces reach and secure the Gazala line, both sides prepare for the next battle

The end of Operation Crusader was to coincide with a series of events that would turn the tide of the war; on 5 December the Red Army counterattacked the German forces on the Eastern Front, the first step of the first major defeat suffered by the German Army so far in that theatre. Two days later, the Japanese attack against Pearl Harbor brought the United States into the war and opened a new front in Asia and the Pacific. In the Mediterranean and the Middle East, the Italian manned-torpedo attack at Alexandria harbour on 19 December 1941 was to once again alter the balance of strength in the area. As was the impending arrival of the German air units that were being transferred from the Eastern Front under the command of Field Marshal Kesselring, with the task of neutralising Malta as an air and naval base.

In spite of Auchinleck's plans to advance further into Tripolitania, the requirements of the new Asian theatre of war and the changing situation in the Mediterranean were to contribute to another swing of the pendulum in the Western Desert. Not only were the British forces under no illusion that, despite their weaknesses, the Axis forces were far from being defeated, the Eighth Army was soon to face the same kind of problems that Rommel had faced while fighting in Cyrenaica: lack of supplies. Only 1,250 tons of supplies could reach the easternmost units in Cyrenaica, 250 tons short of the daily requirement of 1,400 tons. The need to rotate units also led to the 7th Armoured Division being pulled out from the line and replaced with the 1st Armoured Division; the same unit that had been badly mauled in France in 1940 was subsequently

FREE FRENCH FORCES

Apart from the Free French Brigade that fought in the Western Desert in 1942, the Free French also deployed other units from Chad and further south to the Libyan Sahara. These initially consisted of the battalion-sized 'Colonne Leclerc' of January 1941, but one year later were expanded to become regiment-sized units of 900 men.

stripped of its main equipment to supply North Africa before being sent to Egypt and then to Libya, and was still lacking training and cohesion. Since nobody expected that Rommel could be back on the offensive quickly, and given the problems with supply, only the 200th (formerly 22nd) Guards Brigade was deployed facing the enemy at El Agheila, with the 4th Indian Division around Benghazi and the bulk of the 1st Armoured Division deployed west as a reserve.

On 5 January 1942 Rommel got an unexpected gift – a convoy arrived at Tripoli carrying 147 vehicles, 3,500 tons of supplies and fifty-four Panzers. New supplies soon brought the units up to strength, and by 17 January the Italians had eighty-nine medium tanks, while two days later the Germans had ninety-seven Panzers. On 12 January a conference was held by Rommel with his staff, during which the situation at the front was examined. It was clear that the enemy forces facing the Panzergruppe Afrika were weak and lacking experience, for example the 1st Armoured Division. Although they might soon have been strengthened, the Axis forces were superior in strength. After a moment of uncertainty Rommel and his staff agreed that this was the time to attack with 'complete surprise'. The first step was to keep the Italians away from any plans, and they were only informed at the last minute, just as the attack started. Nevertheless, radio intercepts revealed to Eighth Army's HQ that the Germans were up to something, but that there was little cause for immediate concern. On 18 January

Rommel issued his orders, and three days later his second drive into Cyrenaica began.

At 8.30 a.m. on 21 January three columns advanced from the Axis line; to the left Kampfgruppe Marcks (built around the 3rd Reconnaissance Battalion) and the 90th Afrika Division, at the centre the Italian XX Corps (formerly the Corpo d'Armata di Manovra) and to the left the Afrika Korps. Facing weak enemy opposition, the Axis forces progressed with ease and by 11 a.m. on the following day Agedabia was seized, followed six hours later by Antelat. The Germans had broken through. Neither Rommel nor his staff could help wondering what the enemy was up to. Facing the enemy advance, General Godwin-Austen had the 200th Guards Brigade and the 1st Support Group to try to keep control of the main roads and tracks, but since this did not appear to be an attack in force it was soon decided that the best course of action was to pull back the forward units to prevent their encirclement. The movement was started at once, while the 4th Indian Division went to block the via Balbia and the access to Benghazi. On 23 January the greater danger came from the track leading to Msus, the possession of which might have made an encirclement possible. A mistake, an order sent to the wrong German unit, allowed a large number of British troops to withdraw since Saunnu, south-east of Antelat, was not attacked and seized until about 6 p.m. by German troops led personally by Rommel. Facing the bulk of the enemy forces escaping the trap, it was now time for him to plan the next steps.

Rommel now faced a difficult situation, as his Italian allies were not happy with a new drive into Cyrenaica and all its possible consequences, and this resulted in the bulk of the Italian infantry remaining at Mersa Brega to work on fortifications. Furthermore, the enemy was preparing to meet him on the battlefield. On 24 January Godwin-Austen expressed his anxieties to Ritchie about the enemy advance, suggesting a possible withdrawal towards El Mechili, but Ritchie ordered him to concentrate the XIII Corps at Msus, ready to face an enemy attack while covering

Benghazi, which was defended by the 4th Indian Division. Godwin-Austen was authorised to withdraw if necessary anyway, and administrative units were already being evacuated. On 25 January the Afrika Korps attacked Msus, which was seized after a short fight and the capture of 233 prisoners. The only real advantage was that now Rommel had taken into his hands the key position of the whole Western Cyrenaica. Facing the loss of Msus, Godwin-Austen ordered a withdrawal; however, Ritchie halted him and ordered his units to prepare for offensive actions instead, as he believed that the enemy would have overstretched its supply lines once again. Rommel was indeed having fuel problems, having advanced some 250km in five days, but his main aim was to maintain the element of surprise.

During the previous offensives across the desert the Msus–El Mechili line had been used to outflank the enemy forces moving along the coast, and to encircle them before reaching the narrow area on the Gulf of Sirte. Even now, the fact that Rommel's forces were at Msus openly suggested that he was about to attempt a drive across the open desert toward El Mechili, and from there to the coast west of Tobruk, just as he did in 1941. If the 1st Armoured Division caught them in the open, it might have been possible to inflict a great deal of damage. Ritchie's plan seemed to have worked when, on 27 January, British air reconnaissance spotted an enemy column moving from Msus toward El Mechili; Ritchie did not waste time and ordered the 1st Armoured Division at El Charruba to strike the rear of the enemy forces moving toward El Mechili and Benghazi, while the 4th Indian Division was to strike the enemy forces advancing west to Benghazi. 'The enemy has divided his forces, and is weaker than we are in both areas. The keyword is offensive action everywhere.'[23] Rommel would have agreed.

Once again, Rommel was to surprise his enemies; rather than advancing across the desert he decided to attack and seize

---

23   Playfair, *The Mediterranean and the Middle East III*, p. 149

PANZERGRUPPE AND PANZERARMEE

The German Army created four Panzergruppe (Panzer group) commands for the attack against the Soviet Union in 1941. These groups were equivalent to an army and were therefore renamed Panzerarmee, or Panzer army, between the end of 1941 and early 1942.
Panzergruppe Afrika was officially renamed Panzerarmee Afrika on 22 January 1942.

Benghazi with a surprise strike, taking control of the harbour in the process and seizing a large amount of booty to help his supply problems. On 26 January orders were given to Kampfgruppe Marcks and Artillery Command 104 (the former Kampfgruppe Böttcher) to move from Msus to the north-west, seizing the ground just to the south of Benghazi. This was then to be held by the Italian forces and the 90th Afrika Division, advancing along the coast, while the Afrika Korps was to remain at Msus and to feint an attack on El Mechili. The two groups set off on the night of 27/28 January, while a column of the Afrika Korps began the feint attack toward El Mechili. At 11 a.m. on the 28th the German columns were to the south of Benghazi, which was surrounded after four hours of fighting, thus blocking the retreat of 4th Indian Division's 7th Brigade, while the Italian mobile units advanced along the coast to reach Ghemines, just to the south of Benghazi. After bitter fighting Benghazi was seized on 29 January with minimal losses on the German side (fifty-four in all), but a great deal more for the British: about 1,000 prisoners were taken, along with a huge amount of food, ammunition, vehicles and other materiel. On 30 January both sides rested, but Ritchie eventually opted for a withdrawal to the Gazala line, which began almost at once; Rommel's forces followed close by, but were unable to do any damage given their lack of fuel. Godwin-Austen then requested to be relieved of his command

49. A German column on the move; with the arrival of the Afrika Korps the war in the Western Desert became mechanised.

after his disagreements with Ritchie, which he was granted on 2 February. The surprise, speed and success of the German advance was to cause disappointment and concern at all levels of the British commands, exemplified by Godwin-Austen's resignation. This was a bad omen for the future, and out of proportion with the losses suffered during Rommel's second drive into Cyrenaica (about 1,390 troops, and about seventy tanks lost). The British withdrawal was completed by 6 February, and afterwards both sides maintained their positions along the Gazala–Bir Hakeim line to rest, reorganise, refit and prepare for the next battle.

THE LEGACY

There is a common perception that 'Rommel had been beaten, not by British military prowess but by lack of Axis logistic support, and he knew it'.[24] This was not entirely true, for Rommel had also been beaten by his own mistakes and by Auchinleck's determination to bring Crusader to a victorious conclusion, but this view was probably shared by Rommel in the days after he had regained control of Western Cyrenaica, following the bitter defeat during the winter battle.

The fact is that during the first twenty-two months of war in the Western Desert both sides made mistakes, albeit to a varying extent, and while some mistakes were learned from, some were not. A few lessons were learned by all sides during the swinging pendulum that characterised the first months of war, the first one being Tobruk. It was now clear to everybody that control of Tobruk, and especially its harbour, was the key for any other further advances to the extreme west or east of the Western Desert theatre. It was after the seizure of Tobruk on 21–23 January 1941 that O'Connor advanced through the desert to inflict defeat on the Italians at Beda Fomm, and it was thanks to the skilful withdrawal into the Tobruk fortress in April 1941

---

24   Jackson, W.G.F., *The Battle for North Africa 1940–43*, p. 180

that Rommel's first drive into Cyrenaica was halted at the Libyan–Egyptian frontier. With Tobruk firmly in their hands, Wavell and Auchinleck were able to organise offensive actions against the Axis forces, with the clear aim of driving them off from Cyrenaica and advancing once more toward Tripoli. Tobruk turned out to be the hub of the battles fought in the Western Desert, from the first British offensive in December 1940 to Rommel's second drive into Cyrenaica in January–February 1942, and this was clear to every commander and soldier fighting there.

Other lessons, however, were not learned, at least not properly. It was clear that, shortly after the battle of the 'Sunday of the Dead', Auchinleck's original plan for Crusader had turned into a failure; his idea to bring the enemy armour out into the open with the aim of defeating it simply did not work, and the decision to turn Crusader into an infantry battle aimed at relieving Tobruk was – along with Rommel's decision to launch his 'dash to the wire' – the factor that ultimately sealed its fate. This, as well as all the other experiences of fighting the Germans in the open, clearly revealed their tactical superiority in this field and how they were able to inflict serious losses even when facing an enemy superior in numbers, if not in quality. Rommel was well aware of this fact, and it is certainly not by chance that he always tried to fight the enemy in the open, while (particularly after the bitter experiences at Tobruk) avoiding attacks on fortifications and defence lines.

The battle of Gazala, starting with Rommel's attack on 26 May 1942, was to exemplify how both sides learned, or failed to learn, from their previous experiences; following the failure of his plan to outflank Eighth Army's defences, Rommel concentrated his forces in an attempt to open a way across the Gazala defence line, repulsing the British armoured counterattacks one by one. This way he did not repeat the same mistake made during Crusader, i.e. splitting his forces and leaving the initiative to the enemy, and he took advantage of the German superiority in anti-tank guns and unit co-ordination. Conversely, General Ritchie did make the same mistakes that were made during Crusader, when British armoured

50. *Close inspection of a destroyed German Panzer IV tank. Afrika Korps' heavy tank losses at the end of Operation Crusader were mostly due to its retreat, which compelled it to leave behind even repairable tanks.*

units were used piecemeal and were poorly co-ordinated with the infantry, with the result that the Germans used their anti-tank screens to fight the armour off, before counterattacking with their own Panzers. As a result, when finally free to fight again in the open, Rommel defeated the British armour in a battle fought on 12–13 June and, four days later, the Eighth Army withdrew once again to the Libyan–Egyptian frontier.

With the 2nd South African Division defending the Tobruk fortress, there were ominous signs that a repetition of the same events of the previous year would occur. However, this time Rommel concentrated his forces and, enjoying the advantages of a much less determined and skilled enemy, and of weaker defences, he seized Tobruk on 20–21 June 1942. These were the days of glory for Rommel, who was promoted to field marshal on the field, while dark days ensued for the Eighth Army, licking its wounds in Egypt. Yet, Rommel failed to learn from his previous mistakes and overestimated the extent of his victory, just as he did in April 1941 during the drive across Cyrenaica and, once again, in the days following the battle of the 'Sunday of the Dead', when he was unable to resist his obsession with invading Egypt and reaching Alexandria. One month later, Rommel's dreams were crushed by the hard reality at El Alamein, where his forces were unable to break through the tenacious British defence. This was the end of the Axis advance into Egypt, and eventually the place where they would be defeated a few months later. However, there is no doubt where this all started, for the seizure of Tobruk gave Rommel the illusion that the enemy had been defeated and that his advance to Alexandria was possible after all.

It is not by mere chance that, of the many places in which the campaign in the Western Desert was fought, two will stand out more than any other: Tobruk and El Alamein. This is not just because of their strategic importance, or because of the battles fought there, but rather because of their legacies, of victories and of defeats, and of the narrow margins that often separated one from the other. This was the most important legacy of all: the true understanding of how victory or defeat had occurred, and the lessons that were to be learned.

ORDERS OF BATTLE

Operation Compass –
British forces, December
1940 – February 1941

*Commander-in-Chief
Middle East (General Sir
A. Wavell)*

*Western Desert Force
(General R.N. O'Connor)*

    *7th Armoured Division (General
M. O'Moore Creagh)*
        4th Armoured Brigade
        (7th Hussars, 2nd RTR,
        6th RTR)
        7th Armoured Brigade
        (3rd Hussars, 8th Hussars,
        1st RTR)
        7th Support Group (1st
        King's Royal Rifle Corps,
        2nd Rifle Brigade, 1st
        and 4th Royal Horse
        Artillery)
        divisional troops.
        Attached: 7th RTR

    *4th Indian Division (General
N.M. de la Beresford-Peirse)*
        5th Indian Infantry Bri-
        gade (1st Royal Fusiliers,
        3rd/1st Punjab Regiment,
        4th/6th Rajputana Rifles)
        11th Indian Infantry Bri-
        gade (2nd Queen's Own
        Cameron Highlanders,
        1st/6th Rajputana Rifles,
        4th/7th Rajput Regiment)
        divisional troops.
        Attached: 16th British
        Infantry Brigade (1st
        Queen's Royal Regi-
        ment, 2nd Leicestershire
        Regiment, 1st Argyll and
        Sutherland Highlanders)

    *6th Australian Division (General
I. Mackay) – replaced 4th Indian
Division*
        16th Australian Infantry
        Brigade (2nd/1st,
        2nd/2nd, 2nd/3rd
        battalions)
        17th Australian Infantry
        Brigade (2nd/5th,

2nd/6th, 2nd/7th battalions)
19th Australian Infantry Brigade (2nd/4th, 2nd/8th, 2nd/11th battalions), divisional troops

Siege of Tobruk and Operation Battleaxe, April–June 1941

Commander-in-Chief Middle East (General Sir A. Wavell)

XIII Corps (General N.M. de la Beresford-Peirse)

> *7th Armoured Division (General M. O'Moore Creagh)*
>> 4th Armoured Brigade (4th, 7th RTR)
>> 7th Armoured Brigade (2nd, 6th RTR)
>> 7th Support Group (1st King's Royal Rifle Corps, 2nd Rifle Brigade, 1st, 3rd, 4th, 106th Royal Horse Artillery), divisional troops

> *4th Indian Division (General F. Messervy)*
>> 11th Indian Infantry Brigade (2nd Queen's Own Cameron Highlanders, 1st/6th Rajputana Rifles, 2nd/5th Mahrattas)
>> 22nd Guards Brigade (1st Buffs, 2nd Scots Guards, 3rd Coldstream Guards), divisional troops

Tobruk Garrison

> *9th Australian Division (General L.J. Morshead)*
>> 20th Australian Infantry Brigade (2nd/13th, 2nd/15th, 2nd/17th battalions)
>> 24th Australian Infantry Brigade (2nd/28th, 2nd/32nd, 2nd/43rd battalions)
>> 26th Australian Infantry Brigade (2nd/23rd, 2nd/24th, 2nd/48th battalions), divisional troops.
>> Attached: 18th Australian Infantry Brigade (2nd/9th, 2nd/10th, 2nd/12th battalions)
>> 3rd Armoured Brigade (1st, 4th RTR, 1st King's Dragoon Guards, 3rd Queen's Own Hussars, 1st Royal Northumberland Fusiliers)

Afrika Korps (General E. Rommel)

> *5th Light Division (General J. Streich)*
>> 5th Panzer Regiment (two battalions)
>> 200th Infantry Regiment (2nd, 8th Machine Gun battalions)
>> 3rd Reconnaissance Battalion, divisional troops

15th Panzer Division (General
H. von Prittwitz, KIA 10 April
1941, replaced by General
W. Neumann-Silkow)
>8th Panzer Regiment
>(two battalions)
>104th and 115th
>Infantry Regiment (two
>battalions each, at-
>tached: 15th Motorcycle
>Battalion)
>33rd Reconnaissance
>Battalion, divisional
>troops

4th South African Bri-
gade (2nd Royal Durban
Light Infantry, Umvoti
Mounted Rifles, The
Kaffrarian Rifles)
6th South African
Brigade (2nd Transvaal
Scottish, 1st South
African Police, 2nd
South African Police),
divisional troops

Tobruk Garrison

70th Infantry Division (General
R. Scobie)
>14th Infantry Brigade
>(2nd Black Watch, 1st
>Bedfordshire and Hert-
>fordshire, 2nd York and
>Lancaster)
>16th Infantry Brigade
>(2nd King's Own Royals,
>2nd Leicestershire, 2nd
>Queen's Regiment)
>23rd Infantry Brigade
>(1st Durham Light
>Infantry, 4th Border
>Regiment, 1st Essex
>Regiment),
>divisional troops.
>Attached: 32nd Army
>Tank Brigade (1st,
>4th RTR, C Squadron
>1st King's Dragoon
>Guards, D Squadron
>7th RTR)
>1st Polish Carpath-
>ian Brigade (1st, 2nd,
>3rd Carpathian Rifles,
>attached: 11th Czech
>Battalion)

Operation Crusader, 18 November 1941

Commander-in-Chief Middle East (General Sir C. Auchinleck)

Eighth Army (General Sir A. Cunningham, replaced on 26 November by General N. Ritchie)

>Oasis Force (Brigadier D.W. Reid)
>29th Indian Infantry
>Brigade Group (1st
>Worcestershire Regi-
>ment, 3rd/2nd Punjab
>Regiment, 6th/13th
>Frontier Force Rifles)
>6th South African
>Armoured Car Regiment

>2nd South African Division
>(General I. de Villiers) – reserve
>3rd South African
>Brigade (Imperial Light
>Horse, 1st Royal Durban
>Light Infantry, Rand
>Light Infantry)

Orders of Battle

XIII Corps (General A. Godwin-Austen)

4th Indian Division (General F. Messervy)

5th Indian Infantry Brigade (1st Royal Fusiliers, 1st Buffs, 3rd/1st Punjab Regiment)
7th Indian Infantry Brigade (1st Royal Sussex Regiment, 2nd/11th Sikh, 4th/11th Sikh)
11th Indian Infantry Brigade (2nd Queen's Own Cameron Highlanders, 1st/6th Rajputana Rifles, 2nd/5th Mahrattas), divisional troops

2nd New Zealand Division (General B. Freyberg)

4th New Zealand Brigade (18th, 19th, 20th battalions)
5th New Zealand Brigade (21st, 22nd, 23rd battalions)
6th New Zealand Brigade (24th, 25th, 26th battalions)
28 Maori Battalion, Divisional Cavalry Regiment divisional troops

1st Army Tank Brigade (8th, 42nd, 44th RTR)

XXX Corps (General C. Norrie)

7th Armoured Division (General W. Gott)

4th Armoured Brigade (8th Hussars, 3rd, 5th RTR)
7th Armoured Brigade (7th Hussars, 2nd, 6th RTR)
22nd Armoured Brigade (2nd Hussars, 3rd, 4th County of London Yeomanry)
7th Support Group (1st King's Royal Rifle Corps, 2nd Rifle Brigade, 3rd, 4th Royal Horse Artillery), divisional troops

1st South African Division (General G. Brink)

1st South African Brigade (1st Duke of Edinburgh Own's Rifles, 1st Royal Natal Carabineers, 1st Transvaal Scottish)
5th South African Brigade (1st South African Irish Regiment, 2nd Regiment Botha, 3rd Transvaal Scottish), divisional troops

22nd Guards Brigade (becomes 200th Guards Brigade on 14 January 1942) (as 22nd Brigade on 18 November: 3rd Coldstream Guards, 1st Durham Light Infantry)

Panzergruppe Afrika (General E. Rommel)

Afrika Korps (General L. Crüwell)

104th Artillery Command (General K. Böttcher)

151

21st Panzer Division (General General J. von Ravenstein, since 1st December General K. Böttcher)
    5th Panzer Regiment (two battalions)
    104th Infantry Regiment (two infantry battalions, 8th Machine Gun Battalion)
    3rd Reconnaissance Battalion, divisional troops

15th Panzer Division (General W. Neumann-Silkow, since 9 December General G. von Vaerst)
    8th Panzer Regiment (two battalions)
    115th Infantry Regiment (two infantry battalions)
    200th Infantry Regiment (2nd Machine Gun Battalion, 15th Motorcycle Battalion)
    33rd Reconnaissance Battalion, divisional troops

90th 'Afrika' Division (General M. Sümmermann, since 10 December General R. Veith) 25*
    155th Infantry Regiment (three battalions)
    361st 'Afrika' Regiment (two battalions)
    II Battalion of 255th Infantry Regiment,
    III Battalion of 347th Infantry Regiment, 900th Engineer Battalion,

---

* *officially renamed 90th 'Afrika' Division on 28 november 1941. It was previously the 'Afrika' Division.*

    300th 'Oasis' Battalion, divisional troops

Italian Savona Infantry Division (General F. de Giorgis)
    (two infantry regiments with three battalions each, one artillery regiment with three battalions)

Italian XXI Army Corps (General E. Navarrini)

Italian Infantry Divisions: Pavia, Bologna, Brescia, Trento
    (two infantry regiments with three battalions each, one artillery regiment with three battalions)

Italian Corpo d'Armata di Manovra (Manoeuvre Army Corps, General G. Gambara)

Reconnaissance Group
    (two 'Young Fascist' infantry battalions, one armoured car battalion, two light tanks battalions)

Italian Ariete Armoured Division (General M. Balotta)
    132nd tank regiment (three battalions medium tanks)
    32nd tank regiment (three battalions light tanks)
    8th Bersaglieri regiment (light infantry, three battalions), divisional troops

Italian Trieste Motorised Division (General A. Piazzoni)
> 65th, 66th motorised infantry regiments (three battalions each) 9th Bersaglieri regiment (two battalions), divisional troops

FURTHER READING

Agar-Hamilton, J.A.I. and L. Turner, *The Sidi Rezegh Battles, 1941* (1957)

Barnett, Corelli, *The Desert Generals* (1960)

Behrendt, Hans Otto, *Rommel's Intelligence in the Desert Campaign* (1985)

Bharucha, P.C., *North African Campaign* (1956)

Bidwell, Shelford and Dominic Graham, *Firepower. British Army Weapons and Theories of War 1904–1945* (1982)

Buckingham, William F., *Tobruk: The Great Siege, 1941–42* (2008)

Bungay, Stephen, *Alamein* (2002)

Carell, Paul, *The Foxes of the Desert* (1961)

Carver, Michael, *Tobruk* (1964)

———, *Dilemmas of the Desert War* (1986)

Churchill, Sir Winston, *The Second World War. Volume 4: The Hinge of Fate* (1951)

Connell, John, *Auchinleck* (1959)

———, *Wavell: Scholar and Soldier* (1964)

Cumpston, John S., *Rats Remain. Tobruk Siege 1941* (1966)

Ellis, Chris and G. Forty, *Desert Adversaries: 21st Panzer and 7th Armoured Division* (2008)

Ellis, John, *Brute Force. Allied Strategy and Tactics in the Second World War* (1990)

Forty, George, *Afrika Korps at War. Volume 1 – The Road to Alexandria* (1978)

———, *Desert Rats at War. Volume 1 – North Africa* (1975)

Fraser, David, *Knight's Cross. A Life of Field Marshal Erwin Rommel* (1993)

French, David, *Raising Churchill's Army. The British Army and the War Against Germany, 1919–1945* (2000)

Further Reading

Frey, Hellmuth, *Für Rommels Panzer durch die Wüste* (2010)

Greene, Jack and A. Massignani, *Rommel's North African Campaign. September 1940–November 1942* (1994)

Harrison, Frank, *Tobruk. The Great Siege Reassessed* (1999)

Hart, Basil H. Liddell, *The Rommel Papers* (1953)

Heckstall-Smith, Anthony, *Tobruk. Story of a Siege* (1960)

Hinsley, F.H., *British Intelligence in the Second World War: Its Influence on Strategy and Operations. Volume I* (1979)

Irving, David, *The Trail of the Fox. The Life of Field Marshal Erwin Rommel* (1977)

Jackson, W.G.F., *The Battle for North Africa* (1975)

Kitchen, Martin, *Rommel's Desert War. Waging World War II in North Africa, 1941–1943* (2009)

Latimer, Jon, *Tobruk 1941. Rommel's Opening Move* (2004)

Lewin, Ronald, *The Life and Death of the Afrika Korps* (1977)

Long, Gavin, *To Benghazi* (1961)

Lyman, Robert, *The Longest Siege. Tobruk, the Battle that Saved North Africa* (2009)

Maughan, Barton, *Tobruk and El Alamein. Australia in the War of 1939–1945* (1966)

Mellenthin, F.W. von, *Panzer Battles* (1976)

Murphy, W.E., *The Relief of Tobruk. Official History of New Zealand in the Second World War 1939–45* (1961)

Pitt, Barrie, *The Crucible of War. Wavell's Command* (2001)

———, *The Crucible of War. Auchinleck's Command* (2001)

Playfair, I.S.O., *The Mediterranean and the Middle East. Volume I: The Early Successes Against Italy, to May 1941* (1954)

———, *The Mediterranean and the Middle East. Volume II: The Germans Come to the Help of Their Ally, 1941* (1956)

———, *The Mediterranean and the Middle East. Volume III: British Fortunes Reach Their Lowest Ebb* (1960)

Raugh Jr, Harold E., *Wavell in the Middle East, 1939–1941. A Study in Generalship* (1993)

Rebora, Andrea, *Carri Ariete Combattono* (2009)

Stock, James W., *Tobruk. The Siege* (1973)

Taysen, Adalbert von, *Tobruk 1941. Der Kampf in Nordafrika* (1976)

Warner, Philip, *Auchinleck. The Lonely Soldier* (2001)

Wilmot, Chester, *Tobruk 1941. Capture, Siege, Relief* (1945)

At the time of writing, Libya has just emerged from a struggle between Colonel Gaddafi and the rebellion against his regime, which started in Cyrenaica. Tobruk is the easternmost city of the free territory and is still hard to visit (like it had been before). Until recently there was a small museum in Tobruk, located in a Catholic church, where several war relics were kept. As of today, the museums in the United Kingdom offer the widest range of collections related to the Western Desert campaign and to the battle of Tobruk. These include the Imperial War Museum (http://www.iwm.org.uk/), the National Army Museum (http://www.national-army-museum.ac.uk/), and the Royal Artillery Museum (http://www.firepower.org.uk/), all located in the Greater London area, plus the Tank Museum at Bovington, Dorset (http://www.tankmuseum.org/). The Imperial War Museum website has details on the other related museums which are located outside of London, such as Duxford.

There are not many in-depth, well-researched or wide-ranging websites dedicated to the first years of the Western Desert campaign and the battle of Tobruk, with those most frequently occurring on Wikipedia.

Much to the contrary of other battles during the Western Desert and North African campaigns, there are some excellent movies dealing with the battle of Tobruk. The first one to be shot was Charles Chauvel's *The Rats of Tobruk*, produced in Australia in 1944 and distributed in the USA by the RKO, starring Grant Taylor, Peter Finch, Chips Rafferty and George Wallace. Although a wartime propaganda movie, Chauvel's film clearly depicts the siege of 1941 at a personal, ground-level view and is considered a better work than his more famous *Forty Thousand Horsemen* (1940), not to mention the fact that he and his wife actually researched the area for a whole year before production took place. The 1953 movie *The Desert Rats*, directed by Robert Wise and distributed by 20th Century Fox, is rather a post-war Hollywood production which gives a broad view of the battle (which, worth noting, incorrectly used the name given to the British 7th Armoured Division rather than the one adopted by the Australians). The cast included Richard Burton, Robert Newton, James Mason (who was appearing in the role of Rommel again after he played the title role in Henry Hathaway's *Rommel. The Desert Fox* (1951)), Charles Tingwell, Chips Rafferty (probably the only actor to appear in two Tobruk battle movies) and Robert Douglas as the 'general', which is in fact Leslie Morshead. Interestingly, the one movie to be named after Tobruk is not related either to the siege or to the winter battle, as Arthur Hiller's 1967 *Tobruk* actually deals with the September 1942 Commando raid. Related to the 1941 events is Henry Hathaway's 1971 *Raid on Rommel*, showing the story of the ill-fated raid against Rommel's presumed headquarters at Beda Littoria on 13–14 November 1941 (Operation Flipper). The cast includes Richard Burton, John Colicos, Clinton Greyn and Wolfgang Preiss, who replaced Mason in the role of Erwin Rommel. The 2008 Czech production of *Tobruk*, directed by Vaclav Marhoul, with Jan Meduna, Peter Vanek and Matej Hadek amongst others, brought the siege back to the screen after more than half a century. Accurate and well done, the movie again shows the siege at a personal, ground-level view, but this time seen from the perspective of a group of soldiers of the 11th Czech Battalion, attached to the Polish Brigade.

INDEX

Index

Italian East Africa 11–12, 16, 17, 18, 22, 33, 47
Italian units
  Navy 11–12
  Army:
  'Young Fascist' Battalion 127
  Ariete Division 17, 35–36, 49, 50, 55, 71, 85, 87, 89, 102–103, 108, 110, 119–120, 122–127, 129
  Bersaglieri 115
  Blackshirt Divisions 22, 23, 25, 27
  Brescia Division 35–36, 50, 66, 69, 115
  Corpo d'Armata di Manovra (CAM) 50, 85, 130, 140
  Savona Division 134
  Tenth Army 27, 29, 38
  Trento Infantry Division 49–50, 71
  Trieste Infantry Division 49–50, 85, 127, 129
Jalo 89
Jarabub 17, 67, 89
Jebel Akhdar ('Green Mountains') 63–64, 66
Jock columns 59, 118
Kesselring, Field Marshal 138
Keyes, Colonel Geoffrey 84
Kirchheim, General Heinrich 41, 72, 73
Knabe, Colonel Gustav-Georg 42
Knight's Cross 116
Kufra 17, 67
Lamluda 130
Lavarack, General John 66–67
Libya 11–14, 15–19, 21–27, 32, 33, 36, 41, 50, 54, 62, 64, 67, 69, 71, 72, 76, 78, 80, 105, 108, 125, 129, 135, 139, 145–146
Long Range Desert Force 16, 89
M13 tank 31
M3 Stuart ('Honey') Light tank 60, 84, 91, 118, 129, 133
Maaten el Grara 36
Marmon-Herrinton armoured car 99
Marshall-Cornwall, General 39
Matilda tank 25, 27, 28, 45, 48, 60, 68, 73, 75, 79, 81, 84, 100, 112, 136,
McLeish, Corporal Bob 73
Mediterranean Sea 11–13, 20, 21, 24, 46, 52, 78, 110, 113, 125, 138
Mellenthin, Major Friedrich Wilhelm von 44, 108–109
Menny, Colonel Erwin 41
Mersa Brega 17, 20, 34, 128, 133, 140
Mersa Matruh 12, 24–25
Messervy, General 81
Mickl, Colonel Johann 42, 121
Middle East Command 18, 21, 47, 49, 82, 114
Morshead, General Leslie 67–68, 70, 73, 74, 75, 77
Msus 36, 62, 140–142
Murzuk 16, 29
Mussolini, Benito 13, 14, 23, 24, 27, 30
Neame, General Philip 17, 36, 39
Neumann-Silkow, General Walter 41, 103
Norrie, General Charles 41, 89, 106, 109, 113, 114, 125, 126, 134
O'Connor, General Richard 17, 25, 26, 28, 29, 32–33, 36, 39, 45, 59, 144

O'Moore Craigh, General Michael 45
Operation Battleaxe 18, 39, 78, 80–83
Operation Brevity 18, 39, 78, 83
Operation Compass 16, 25, 26, 59, 104, 137
Operation Crusader 14, 19, 40, 41, 47, 48, 53, 58, 60, 79, 82, 85, 87, 89, 90, 92, 109, 111, 127, 128, 133, 138, 144–146
Operation Flipper 19, 84
Panzer I tank 61
Panzer II tank 35, 61
Panzer III tank 61, 94, 104, 137
Panzer IV tank 61, 102, 111, 137, 146
Paulus, General Friedrich 71, 73, 76
Point 175 92, 114, 119–122, 125
Point 178 98, 120–121
Pope, General Vyvian 41
Pour le Mérite (the Blue Max) 43, 44
Prittwitz, Heinrich von 41, 66, 69
Ras el Medauar 69, 71–73, 76
Ravenstein, General Johann von 42, 121
Rawlings, Corporal Bill 96
Rebora, Lieutenant Andrea 55–56, 107
Ritchie, General Neil 41, 106, 114, 125–126, 128, 130–133, 140–143, 145
Rommel, Field Marshal Erwin 17, 19, 33–37, 38–39, 41–44, 46–47, 50, 66, 69, 71–73, 76, 80–82, 84, 86, 91–93, 95, 98, 101, 105, 107–114, 118–123, 125–127, 128–136, 138–143, 144–147
Sahara Desert 16, 17, 64, 67, 139
Saunnu 140
Schorm, Lieutenant Joachim 34
Scobie, General 116
SdKfz 250/3 command vehicle 126
Sidi Azeiz 78, 91, 97, 111–113, 117–118
Sidi Barrani 12–13, 15, 16, 23–25, 27, 80, 82
Sidi Omar 27, 78–79, 81, 83, 89, 90, 92, 100, 106, 108–109, 111–112, 117
Sidi Rezegh 64, 83, 87, 90, 92, 94–95, 97–99, 102–104, 106, 108, 110, 113–115, 117–121, 123–124, 128
Sollum 16, 17, 18, 20, 50, 63, 76, 79, 80, 92, 108–109, 111, 117–118, 129, 134, 136,
Soluch 36, 131
S mmermann, General Max 42, 130
Sterling, Captain David 85
Streich, General Johannes 34, 42, 43, 66, 108–109
Tellera, General Giuseppe 38
'Tiger' convoy 8, 78
Tmimi 66, 85, 129
Tripoli 29, 33, 110, 123, 139, 145
Vaerst, General Gustav von 41
Valentine tank 27, 60, 84, 136
Veith, General Richard 42
'Via Balbia' coastal road 64, 70, 109, 126, 130, 140
Victoria Cross 123
Ward VC, 2nd Lieutenant G., 123
Wavell, General Archibald 18, 21, 24–26, 33, 35, 39, 40, 47, 49, 66, 80–82, 145
Western Desert Force 25, 28, 39, 45, 69, 82
Westphal, Colonel Siegfried 44, 107–109, 117
Wilson, General Sir Henry Maitland 39
Zanfran 119, 122–124

EXPLORE HISTORY'S MAJOR CONFLICTS WITH
BATTLE STORY